Mastering Symfony

Orchestrate the designing, development, testing, and
deployment of web applications with Symfony

Sohail Salehi

BIRMINGHAM - MUMBAI

Mastering Symfony

First published: April 2016

Production reference: 1210416

Published by Packt Publishing Ltd.
Livery Place
35 Livery Street
Birmingham B3 2PB, UK.

ISBN 978-1-78439-031-0

www.packtpub.com

Credits

Author
Sohail Salehi

Reviewers
Mickaël Andrieu

Vincent COMPOSIEUX

Tito Miguel Costa

Commissioning Editor
Usha Iyer

Acquisition Editors
Tushar Gupta

Richard Harvey

Content Development Editor
Aishwarya Pandere

Technical Editors
Pranil Pathare

Danish Shaikh

Copy Editor
Tasneem Fatehi

Project Coordinator
Nidhi Joshi

Proofreader
Safis Editing

Indexer
Mariammal Chettiyar

Production Coordinator
Nilesh Mohite

Cover Work
Nilesh Mohite

About the Author

Sohail Salehi is a full stack web developer who is constantly seeking creative solutions for complex problems. He believes that what has been taught as universalities should be considered as a basic stepping stone to real-life challenges. They cannot be used as practical solutions. He learned that a one-size-fits-all solution does not work in the IT world. Every business, every coding challenge, and every environment setup has its own signature and requires some tweaking on basic principals to make sure that it receives a reliable cost-effective solution.

When he is not staring at his computer screen, he is watching sunsets and sunrises, swimming and surfing in the ocean, and putting his subconscious mind at work by asking creative questions while facing life's ups and downs on a daily basis.

I would like to thank the Packt Publishing team for being supportive at all times and also being patient with me at the times I've gone wild and updated the book contents over and over again.

About the Reviewers

Mickaël Andrieu is a passionate open source engineer, contributor, and maintainer of projects such as Symfony, CasperJS, and Certificationy. He is currently a core developer and technical evangelist of the open source e-commerce solution, PrestaShop, built around the Symfony framework in its latest version. An ex-developer at SensioLabs, he has accumulated good expertise in PHP and the Symfony framework.

When he is not working on his own project, he teaches best development practices to engineering students or advices big companies on their open source strategies.

He has worked at SensioLabs and Lp digital system.

He will probably be working on another book, as Llewellyn F. Rozario just contacted him for another review.

Vincent COMPOSIEUX is a French web engineer who loves technologies such as PHP, Python, NodeJS, and Go. He is based in Paris and working at Ekino, a French web agency that focuses on quality.

Previously, he has worked for e-commerce companies and web agencies on multiple web projects with high traffic.

He loves web technologies and frameworks and has experience using the Zend framework, Magento, and Symfony.

He has great experience of Symfony because he has been using it since the very first version and is actively involved in the Symfony community.

Indeed, he has developed some bundles such as `FeedBundle` to manage RSS and Atom feeds, `GoogleTranslateBundle` to use the Google Translate API to translate content, and some others. He is also a contributor to the Sonata bundles suite.

You can contact him and see more on his personal website, `http://vincent.composieux.fr`.

Tito Miguel Costa is a full stack web application developer with over 10 years of experience in PHP. He started using Symfony back in 2007, when version 1.0 was released and it remains his favorite framework until now. Back in Portugal, where he is originally from, he organized several courses and oriented a dissertation on how to optimize and scale projects built with Symfony. Currently, he maintains several open source bundles and works as a senior Symfony developer at Lendable, one of the most promising start-ups in London.

www.PacktPub.com

eBooks, discount offers, and more

Did you know that Packt offers eBook versions of every book published, with PDF and ePub files available? You can upgrade to the eBook version at www.PacktPub.com and as a print book customer, you are entitled to a discount on the eBook copy. Get in touch with us at customercare@packtpub.com for more details.

At www.PacktPub.com, you can also read a collection of free technical articles, sign up for a range of free newsletters and receive exclusive discounts and offers on Packt books and eBooks.

https://www2.packtpub.com/books/subscription/packtlib

Do you need instant solutions to your IT questions? PacktLib is Packt's online digital book library. Here, you can search, access, and read Packt's entire library of books.

Why subscribe?

- Fully searchable across every book published by Packt
- Copy and paste, print, and bookmark content
- On demand and accessible via a web browser

Table of Contents

Preface	**vii**
Chapter 1: Installing and Configuring Symfony	**1**
Why Symfony?	**1**
Influenced by Symfony	2
How bright is the future?	3
Installation	**4**
Composer and Packagist	**6**
Installing Symfony via Composer	9
The road map	11
Checking the installation	12
Summary	**12**
Chapter 2: The Request and Response Life Cycle	**13**
The big picture	**13**
Anatomy of a bundle	**16**
Generating a new bundle	18
Best practices	21
Custom bundles versus AppBundle	**22**
Creating templates with TWIG	**23**
Controller/View interaction	24
Conditional templates	25
Make it dynamic	26
Database configurations	26
Generating an entity	27
Installing bundles created by others	29
Creating data fixtures	**30**
Loading data fixtures	31

Dynamic templates and controllers	**32**
The big picture with MVC	**34**
Summary	**35**
Chapter 3: Setting Up the Environment	**37**
The importance of Continuous Integration	**38**
Amazon Web Services	**38**
Elastic Compute Cloud	**40**
Creating a new instance	41
Setting up the server	**45**
Installing Apache	45
Installing MySQL and PHP	45
Installing Jenkins	46
Setting up security and installing plugins in Jenkins	48
Simple Email Service	**53**
Configuring Jenkins	55
Installing PHP tools	**56**
Sniff Symfony codes	58
Orchestrating the build process	**58**
Creating a new job in Jenkins	**64**
Running the first build	**69**
How does GitHub alert Jenkins about new pushes?	70
Do I need CI?	**72**
Summary	**73**
Chapter 4: Using Behavior-Driven Development in Symfony	**75**
Getting started with BDD	**76**
Is BDD a replacement for TDD?	76
What is Behat?	**77**
Installing and configuring Behat	77
The features we need for this project	78
More information about the project	79
Gherkin – the common language	80
Writing a scenario for the about page	**81**
Seeing it in action	81
Headless versus zombie	83
Using the Selenium2 controller for automated tests	83
The about page does not follow BDD	**85**
A scenario to show the user's details	85
Implementing the user's details scenario	88
Testing the scenario	89
More about the acceptance test flow in Mink	**90**

Defining and prioritizing features **91**
Codeception – the BDD style testing framework **92**
Installing the Codeception framework 93
Bootstrapping Codeception 93
Test suits 95
The testers 97
Adding sample tests 98
Running the tests 99
Summary **101**

Chapter 5: Business Logic **103**
Choosing between creating a Model or entity **104**
So where does the business logic live? **106**
Reviewing the facts and building entity relationships **106**
Creating ERDs using MySQL Workbench 107
Adding a new entity 109
Adding a new relationship 111
Creating actual tables from a diagram 112
Generating entities 115
Data fixtures 116
Some business logic features and scenarios **120**
TDD and BDD with Codeception **121**
Step one – creating a functional test 122
Developing the missing code 123
Step two – creating the unit tests 124
Setting up the database for a test environment in the right way 125
Dropping and recreating the database for each test 126
Creating unit tests 127
Writing the code to pass the test 130
Running functional and unit tests 131
Step three – creating an acceptance test 132
On the CI side of the story **134**
Summary **135**

Chapter 6: Dashboard and Security **137**
How security is organized in Symfony? **138**
Authentication 139
Authorization 140
Handling users with FOSUserBundle **140**
Security settings 142
Adding the required configurations to FOSUserBundle 143
Adding routes 143

Updating the tables   144
A simple road test   145
Generating automated data fixtures   **147**
Introducing AliceBundle   147
Creating data fixtures with Alice   148
Relationship with Alice   149
Setting up the login redirection   150
Creating tests for the new controller   151
Creating the Dashboard Controller   152
Securing the dashboard   154
The Sonata project   **154**
Installing and configuring Sonata bundle   155
Adding contents to the dashboard   156
Creating admin feature for entities with relations   159
Integrating FOSUserBundle into the admin area   **160**
Installing SonataUserBundle   160
SonataUserBundle configuration   161
Updating the routes   162
Setting the security   164
Checking the installation   165
Putting SonataUserBundle in charge   166
User dashboard   **169**
Generating CRUD   **169**
Modifying the forms   171
Summary   **172**
Chapter 7: The Presentation Layer   **173**
How assets are organized   **173**
Asset management   **174**
How templates are organized   **175**
Let's mold the clay   **176**
To navigate or not to navigate   **179**
What is Bootstrap?   **180**
MopaBootstrapBundle   **180**
Bootstrap configuration   182
Creating your first menu   **184**
Rendering the menu in a template   186
The Dashboard template   **186**
Overriding templates   **188**
Profile-related templates   188
Changing the backend logo   **191**
Summary   **192**

Chapter 8: Project Review   193
The dashboard's contents   193
Visual blocks that provide statistics about tasks   194
A feature file for the finished tasks block   195
Implementing the finished tasks block   197
Implementing the dashboard controller   200
Uploading files with SonataMediaBundle   201
Adding an attachment feature to the Task entity   202
Team and team members   203
The Team entity   204
Adding a notification system   207
Adding time tracking properties   208
The notification business logic   210
Events, event dispatchers, and event listeners   212
The Notifier event listener   213
Summary   215

Chapter 9: Services and Service Containers   217
How to create a service   218
How are services beneficial to our projects?   218
How to call a service   219
How to configure a service   220
Why is it called a Dependency Injection Container?   220
Why didn't we import services inside the bundle?   222
How to create and load services via autowiring   223
Organizing services with tags   224
Summary   225

Chapter 10: Custom User Commands   227
Creating and registering commands   227
Creating commands for tasks   228
The configuration part   229
The execution part   230
Adding interactivity to commands   233
Console helpers   233
Summary   238

Chapter 11: More about Dev, Test and Prod Environments   239
Why do we need different environments?   239
The environment configuration file   240
Processing configuration files   240
Creating a new environment   242
The config file   242

The front controller	244
Summary	**244**
Chapter 12: Caching in Symfony	**245**
Definition of a cache	**245**
Characteristics of a good cache	247
Caches in a Symfony project	**248**
Key players in the HTTP cache header	**250**
Using the Symfony reverse proxy cache	**251**
Set expiration for dashboard page	252
Validation strategy	256
How to mix expiration and validation strategies	**257**
Doctrine cache	258
Putting it all together	**260**
ESI for selective caching	**261**
Sophisticated bundles	**262**
Summary	**262**
Index	**263**

Preface

Welcome to your journey in *Mastering Symfony*. It is my duty and absolute pleasure to show you a different side of Symfony's world and take your development knowledge to a whole new level. In this book, I will not only sharpen your Symfony skills, but will also show you how to look at a project from different angles.

As a backend developer, you can always stick to your skill set and deliver a good job. However, it would be excellent if we could experience the way a business requirement is born, how a project manager sees the problem, what kind of technologies a system administrator uses to host the project, and how it affects developers, before finally knowing how to establish a more efficient work flow with frontend developers.

Having already published a few books, I am proud to say that this one—*Mastering Symfony*—is unique. After warming you up with some introductory materials, I will take you to the heart of the devil and show you how to find your way around a seriously robust project with mountains of real-life challenges. To run this show properly, I needed a decent-size stage. That's why I've decided to build a project management web application over the tutorials of this book. This web application gives me enough space to explore and expand many of Symfony's features required for my goal.

After the two introductory chapters, I will talk about how to set up a project properly. In other words, I will discuss the importance of concepts such as version control, continuous integration, deployment process, behavior-driven development, and so on. I will use Amazon Web Services to host our development, test, and deployment servers and show you how to integrate AWS tools and technologies into your Symfony project.

Then, I will talk about why the development culture has changed recently and why, before writing a single line of code, we have to be clear about scenarios and behaviors. I will discuss Behat and Mink and, more importantly, show you how to utilize them in your projects.

Finally, after I feel confident about everything being in the right place, we will start the real coding. In our Model layer, we will create business logic via Doctrine and feed it with data fixtures. In our Controller layer, we will develop and use a dozen of amazing functionalities coming from various bundles, and in our View layer, we will explore the Twig template engine thoroughly and implement slick frontend features and mobile functionality with the Bootstrap 3.x framework.

A good web app should be able to provide decent security, a user-friendly dashboard, and reasonable speed. That's where I will expand the security concept in Symfony and discuss the Sonata project, followed by the idea of CMF. For those who concern themselves with performance, I will show you how to create blazing fast Symfony applications with the help of reverse proxy caching systems such as Varnish.

What this book covers

Chapter 1, *Installing and Configuring Symfony*, helps you understand the idea of packages and package management along with the installation of Symfony.

Chapter 2, *The Request and Response Life Cycle*, introduces you to basic Symfony concepts such as bundles, routing, twig, doctrine, and so on over the course of a request/response life cycle.

Chapter 3, *Setting Up the Environment*, shows you how to set up development, test, and deployment environments in AWS and set up Behat and Git for BDD and version control respectively.

Chapter 4, *Using Behavior-Driven Development in Symfony*, covers Behat and Mink and how to use them to create reliable projects.

Chapter 5, *Business Logic*, discusses the model layer and Doctrine thoroughly.

Chapter 6, *Dashboard and Security*, shows you authentication and authorization steps in a security checking process and how to create a control panel for our project using the Sonata project and its bundles. The FOSUserBundle will be explained as well.

Chapter 7, *The Presentation Layer*, discusses the Twig template engine and Bootstrap 3.x framework. We will see how to use a bundle to integrate Bootstrap into our templates.

Chapter 8, *Project Review*, reviews what we have created so far and optimizes the code further.

Chapter 9, Services and Service Containers, explains concepts such as Dependency Injection, Service Containers, and Services.

Chapter 10, Custom User Commands, walks you through the steps to create customized commands for Symfony's console.

Chapter 11, More about Dev, Test, and Prod Environments, is a short chapter about Symfony environments. We will see how different they are from each other, how we can customize them based on project requirements, and how to create our own environments with their own front controller.

Chapter 12, Caching in Symfony, talks about performance optimization and the usage of Varnish and Memcached in our project.

What you need for this book

Although examples of this book can be adapted and executed on any machine, my headspace is mainly around Linux and OSX platforms. For a deeper focus on the subject itself, I would suggest a Windows user to install Linux via a virtual machine such as Oracle's VirtualBox and follow the samples in a Linux environment. In *Chapter 3, Setting Up the Environment*, we will need an AWS account. Thanks to Amazon, there is a *1-year free tier* account, which gives us enough resources to follow examples in this book. Before installing Symfony, make sure that you have the latest stable version of PHP and MySQL installed already. Having a database management application such as MySQL Workbench, HeidiSQL, or NaviCat is optional but it is nice to have them.

Who this book is for

This book is for PHP developers who have already used Symfony and are looking to master the framework to its fullest potential. In other words, I presume that you have been using PHP and object-oriented techniques for a while and are familiar with Symfony basics already. To make sure that we are on the same page, I will give you a crash course at the beginning of this book; then we will explore more advanced topics as we proceed.

Conventions

In this book, you will find a number of styles of text that distinguish between different kinds of information. Here are some examples of these styles, and an explanation of their meaning.

Code words in text are shown as follows: "We can inherit other templates through the use of the `extends()` tag."

A block of code is set as follows:

```
public function aboutAction($name)
{
    $em = $this->container->get('doctrine')->getManager();
    $repo = $em->getRepository('ProjectBundle:Assignee');
    $photographer = $repo->findOneBy(array('name' =>$name));
    return $this->render('ProjectBundle:Default:about.html.twig',
                         array('Assignee' =>$Assignee));
}
```

When we wish to draw your attention to a particular part of a code block, the relevant lines or items are set in bold:

```
public function aboutAction($name)
{
    $em = $this->container->get('doctrine')->getManager();
    $repo = $em->getRepository('ProjectBundle:Assignee');
    $photographer = $repo->findOneBy(array('name' =>$name));
    return $this->render('ProjectBundle:Default:about.html.twig',
                         array('Assignee' =>$Assignee));
}
```

Any command-line input or output is written as follows:

```
app/console doctrine:fixtures:load --append
```

New terms and **important words** are shown in bold. Words that you see on the screen, in menus or dialog boxes for example, appear in the text like this: "in Symfonyprofiler page click on the **Security** button to see if the current user is authenticated".

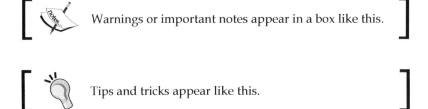

> Warnings or important notes appear in a box like this.

> Tips and tricks appear like this.

Reader feedback

Feedback from our readers is always welcome. Let us know what you think about this book—what you liked or disliked. Reader feedback is important for us as it helps us develop titles that you will really get the most out of.

To send us general feedback, simply e-mail feedback@packtpub.com, and mention the book's title in the subject of your message.

If there is a topic that you have expertise in and you are interested in either writing or contributing to a book, see our author guide at www.packtpub.com/authors.

Customer support

Now that you are the proud owner of a Packt book, we have a number of things to help you to get the most from your purchase.

Downloading the example code

You can download the example code files for this book from your account at http://www.packtpub.com. If you purchased this book elsewhere, you can visit http://www.packtpub.com/support and register to have the files e-mailed directly to you.

You can download the code files by following these steps:

1. Log in or register to our website using your e-mail address and password.
2. Hover the mouse pointer on the **SUPPORT** tab at the top.
3. Click on **Code Downloads & Errata**.
4. Enter the name of the book in the **Search** box.
5. Select the book for which you're looking to download the code files.
6. Choose from the drop-down menu where you purchased this book from.
7. Click on **Code Download**.

You can also download the code files by clicking on the **Code Files** button on the book's webpage at the Packt Publishing website. This page can be accessed by entering the book's name in the **Search** box. Please note that you need to be logged in to your Packt account.

Once the file is downloaded, please make sure that you unzip or extract the folder using the latest version of:

* WinRAR / 7-Zip for Windows
* Zipeg / iZip / UnRarX for Mac
* 7-Zip / PeaZip for Linux

Downloading the color images of this book

We also provide you with a PDF file that has color images of the screenshots/ diagrams used in this book. The color images will help you better understand the changes in the output. You can download this file from `https://www.packtpub. com/sites/default/files/downloads/MasteringSymfony_ColorImages.pdf`.

Errata

Although we have taken every care to ensure the accuracy of our content, mistakes do happen. If you find a mistake in one of our books—maybe a mistake in the text or the code—we would be grateful if you could report this to us. By doing so, you can save other readers from frustration and help us improve subsequent versions of this book. If you find any errata, please report them by visiting `http://www.packtpub. com/submit-errata`, selecting your book, clicking on the **Errata Submission Form** link, and entering the details of your errata. Once your errata are verified, your submission will be accepted and the errata will be uploaded to our website or added to any list of existing errata under the Errata section of that title.

To view the previously submitted errata, go to `https://www.packtpub.com/books/ content/support` and enter the name of the book in the search field. The required information will appear under the **Errata** section.

Piracy

Piracy of copyrighted material on the Internet is an ongoing problem across all media. At Packt, we take the protection of our copyright and licenses very seriously. If you come across any illegal copies of our works in any form on the Internet, please provide us with the location address or website name immediately so that we can pursue a remedy.

Please contact us at `copyright@packtpub.com` with a link to the suspected pirated material.

We appreciate your help in protecting our authors and our ability to bring you valuable content.

Questions

If you have a problem with any aspect of this book, you can contact us at `questions@packtpub.com`, and we will do our best to address the problem.

1
Installing and Configuring Symfony

This chapter is merely a refresher for those who are pretty confident in using Symfony and an introduction for those who are quick learners! You can expect to read about how to install the Symfony Standard Edition package and manage its dependencies via Composer. After installation, we will check to make sure that everything is configured properly. The following are the main topics that we will talk about in this chapter:

- Discussing Symfony
- Using Composer and Packagist
- Installing Symfony
- Checking the installation
- Running a PHP built-in web server

Why Symfony?

I don't like to talk about features, numbers, and statistics. I don't do detailed comparisons between frameworks as well. Instead, I'd like to share an experience with you. As a PHP developer, I worked for the New Zealand Herald newspaper for a while. Sure, they are not the oldest newspaper in the world, but in 2013, they celebrated their 150th anniversary, which makes it very clear that over the years, they have created layers and layers of code on top of each other and used or tried almost every framework and technology in their website and internal newspaper systems. Their repositories contain tons of legacy codes written in different languages. You won't believe it if I say different parts of their system were implemented in Perl, Java, C#, ColdFusion, and PHP, and there was (perhaps, still is?) an API layer that acts as a communicating bridge between all of them.

Due to many factors such as maintenance costs, in the past few years, people at the NZ Herald decided to migrate their entire applications and services into one integrated system; something that is reliable, efficient, and easy to expand and maintain. Having experienced many frameworks already, the solution architects at NZ Herald chose Symfony as their framework.

They realized that those colorful graphs and pretty pictures that compare benchmarking results for various frameworks are worth nothing when it comes to real-life problems. They experienced the efficiency of various frameworks in the day-to-day challenges and understood that no matter how fast the development speed might look at the beginning, the most important thing is how reliable it actually is and how much it costs when it comes to maintaining the project. They simply put a price tag on many factors including performance, abstraction, decouplement, portability, integration, and above all, how well organized the code base will be after spending several years and using several men for the development. Guess what? Symfony beat every PHP framework out there.

What I'm trying to say is that Symfony is not just another tool for web app or website development. It is a new culture for web development, a solid reliable foundation that you can build your project on top of with peace of mind. I call it a new culture because for the first time, I see that it has made various PHP communities talk to each other and work together. I believe this is the most important PHP achievement ever. In the years to come, we will see more about this movement.

Influenced by Symfony

I believe one of the main reasons why Symfony stands out of the crowd is the way it defines the **Model-View-Controller (MVC)** design pattern. This is the key: Symfony defines MVC while many other frameworks try to simply follow MVC rules. Can you see the difference? This means that Symfony contains MVC but does not constrain it. Have a look at the MVC definition and keep it in mind that as we continue the journey through the chapters of this book, you will see what I mean by this. Maybe, this is reason that other PHP frameworks and **Content Management Systems (CMS)** adapted the Symfony components and started to follow in its footsteps.

If you look at the following link, you will see the other great players such as Drupal, phpBB, Laravel, Composer, Doctrine, Behat, and many others who use and benefit from Symfony components:

```
http://symfony.com/projects
```

For those who concern themselves with performance and their judgment is blinded by *Hello World* benchmarking results, I can talk about large companies such as BBC, CBS, and many others who chose Symfony.

Please don't tell me that these big boys didn't do due diligence before making a big decision like choosing a framework. They know the amount of pressure their website receives on a hourly basis and they do care about the quality of their service. There must be a good reason that they chose Symfony over other frameworks. In a nutshell, Symfony helps have a better organized code that reduces the maintenance costs tremendously and, at the same time, it can benefit from modern caching systems such as Varnish, which help with a better performance. *Chapter 12, Caching in Symfony* is all about performance improvement and caching systems.

How bright is the future?

In December 2013, when Fabien Potencier—the creator of Symfony—announced that he raised seven million dollars to boost Symfony and its ecosystem, I literally dropped other frameworks and decided to invest and focus even more on Symfony.

It is clear to me if he was capable of making his mark without raising money, then from 2014 onwards, he will be able to make a huge impact on the PHP world.

Don't get me wrong; I've been using other frameworks and respect other teams who made an effort to create a web development tool with PHP. I have used famous frameworks such as Zend to domestic packages such as MySource Matrix and SilverStripe. As a hobbyist, I also try new libraries and ideas in the open source world. However, every PHP developer needs to choose a right direction and set of tools as his main weapon. For me, it is Symfony, and I can see that Symfony developers will be in even higher demand soon.

 Assuming that you are an experienced PHP developer and familiar with open source development, the tutorials in this book are provided for Linux and Mac platforms. I politely invite Windows users to install a VM application such as Oracle VirtualBox and any Linux distribution to follow the provided examples. You can download it from https://www.virtualbox.org/.

Installation

There are four ways to install the Symfony framework:

- Download the archive file in the root of our project and unpack it there
- Clone the project from GitHub
- Use the Symfony installer tool
- Use Composer to install it for us

The easiest way is to download the Symfony installer and make it publicly accessible via the following commands:

```
$ sudo curl -LsS https://symfony.com/installer -o /usr/local/bin/symfony
$ sudo chmod a+x /usr/local/bin/symfony
```

Now create a new project simply by running the following command:

```
$ symfony new mava
```

As this command shows, it will ask the Symfony installer to create a new folder in the current path called mava, and when you hit enter, you will see that the Symfony source code will be downloaded to that folder:

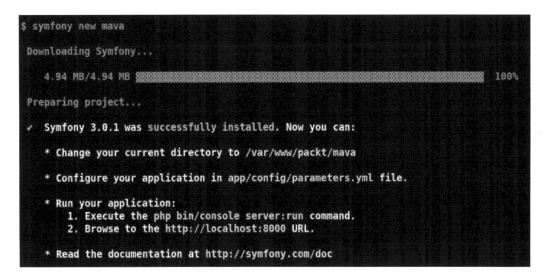

 If you don't mention a version number or branch name in the installer command, it downloads and installs the latest stable version of Symfony.

In the list of things that we can do after installation is running the application immediately, without installing a virtual host. Thanks to the PHP built-in web server, we can run it via Symfony's console and browse the **mava** app at port 8000 on localhost:

```
$ bin/console server:run
```

The following screenshot shows how http://localhost:8000 looks like in your favourite browser:

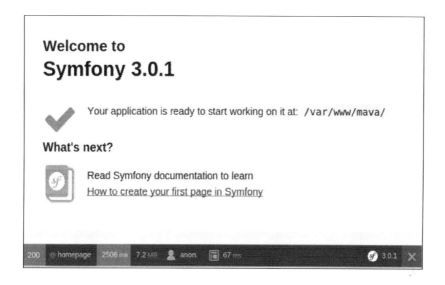

Downloading the example code

You can download the example code files for this book from your account at http://www.packtpub.com. If you purchased this book elsewhere, you can visit http://www.packtpub.com/support and register to have the files e-mailed directly to you.

You can download the code files by following these steps:

- Log in or register to our website using your e-mail address and password.
- Hover the mouse pointer on the **SUPPORT** tab at the top.
- Click on **Code Downloads & Errata**.
- Enter the name of the book in the **Search** box.
- Select the book for which you're looking to download the code files.
- Choose from the drop-down menu where you purchased this book from.
- Click on **Code Download**.

You can also download the code files by clicking on the **Code Files** button on the book's webpage at the Packt Publishing website. This page can be accessed by entering the book's name in the **Search** box. Please note that you need to be logged in to your Packt account.

Once the file is downloaded, please make sure that you unzip or extract the folder using the latest version of:

- WinRAR / 7-Zip for Windows
- Zipeg / iZip / UnRarX for Mac
- 7-Zip / PeaZip for Linux

Composer and Packagist

Composer is a dependency manager application that can be used to install PHP packages.

Some developers prefers Composer, not just because it is easy to use, but it is far more efficient when it comes to keeping track of the project dependencies. In fact, the main reason for creating Composer was to provide a reliable and consistent environment to develop PHP projects.

Imagine a team of PHP developers who work on the same project using various libraries and resources. Sometimes, it can be a nightmare if updating an existing library or installing a new one crashes the code of another developer in the team. Someone should be in charge of tracking all dependencies and controlling the updates and installs to make sure that the project development runs smoothly. In the past, that person used to be the lead developer, but thanks to Composer, the dependency management during development, staging, and production phases is handled automatically by Composer.

Let's get started by downloading Composer if you don't have it already:

```
$ curl -sS https://getcomposer.org/installer | php
```

I presume that you have already installed the latest stable version of PHP and required extensions and libraries including **curl**. In case you don't have curl, you can install Composer via the following command:

```
$ php -r "readfile('https://getcomposer.org/
installer');" | php
```

Move it to your /usr/local/bin folder so that it is accessible from everywhere in your machine:

```
$ sudo mv composer.phar /usr/local/bin/composer
```

Depending on the distribution of your Linux, this path might be /usr/bin instead. Use the echo $PATH command to find out about the location.

Composer is just a manager. It does not store any libraries or packages in itself. However, it works very closely with a package repository called **Packagist** to make sure that it gets the right packages with the correct dependencies. To do so, Packagist talks to Composer via a configuration file called composer.json, which contains many settings including dependency information.

Symfony Standard Edition is a package saved in `https://packagist.org/`. Go to the website and search `symfony` and you will see the Symfony framework along with a list of Symfony components as the search result:

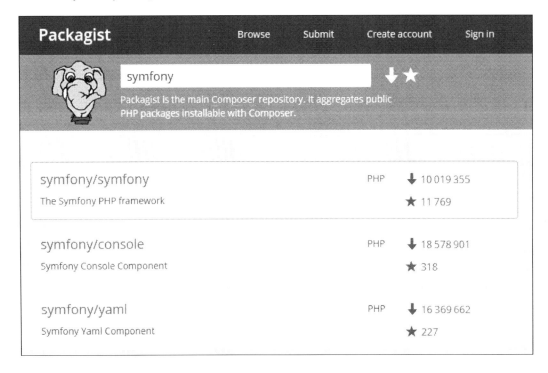

In this book, we will deal mainly with three Composer commands:

- `$ composer create-project [package] [/path] [version]`: This creates a brand new project by downloading a specific version of a package to the specified directory
- `$ composer install`: This installs a package and fetches all the dependent packages to your project
- `$ composer update`: This updates the current packages

Let's see how to install the Symfony Standard Edition package via Composer.

 Did you know that with the self-update option, you can upgrade the Composer to the latest stable version?

`$ composer self-update`

Installing Symfony via Composer

Fire a terminal and go to /var/www. I chose to install Symfony there to keep it simple and avoid different usernames and folders. Create a new folder called mava and set the ownership to yourself:

```
$ cd /var/www
$ sudo mkdir mava
$ sudo chown -hR <YourUserName>:<YourUserName> mava
```

Now type the following command:

```
$ composer create-project symfony/symfony mava/
```

As you can see in the following image, version 3.0.1 is the latest stable version. We can always choose a long-term support version if we want to take a conservative approach toward a project or we can choose the development version if we are crazy enough to ask for everything cutting-edge. Normal people like me always choose the latest stable version. In other words, it is a trade-off between the latest features and longest support:

If the installation process runs smoothly, you will see a bunch of packages being downloaded and installed to the /mava directory:

```
Using version ^3.0 for symfony/symfony
./composer.json has been updated
Loading composer repositories with package information
Updating dependencies (including require-dev)
  - Installing psr/log (1.0.0)
    Loading from cache


  - Installing doctrine/lexer (v1.0.1)
```

```
      Loading from cache

    - Installing doctrine/annotations (v1.2.7)
      Loading from cache

    - Installing doctrine/collections (v1.3.0)
      Loading from cache

    - Installing doctrine/cache (v1.6.0)
      Loading from cache

    - Installing doctrine/inflector (v1.1.0)
      Loading from cache

    - Installing doctrine/common (v2.6.1)
      Loading from cache
etc...
```

After Composer has finished downloading and unpacking all the dependencies, it will ask a couple of questions including sample demo, database settings, and mailer settings. Just accept the default answer by pushing *Enter*:

```
Creating the "app/config/parameters.yml" file
Some parameters are missing. Please provide them.
database_driver (pdo_mysql):
database_host (127.0.0.1):
database_port (null):
database_name (symfony):
database_user (root):
database_password (null):
mailer_transport (smtp):
mailer_host (127.0.0.1):
mailer_user (null):
mailer_password (null):
locale (en):
secret (ThisTokenIsNotSoSecretChangeIt):
debug_toolbar (true):
debug_redirects (false):
use_assetic_controller (true):
```

These settings will be saved in the `app/config/parameters.yml` file, and we always have a chance to change them later. If everything was okay, at the end, the cache will be cleared and the default assets will be installed as follows:

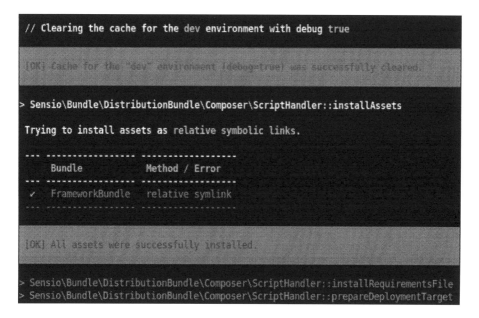

The road map

If you are concerned about how long your choice of the Symfony version is going to be supported, visit the `http://symfony.com/roadmap` page, scroll down, enter the version number, and push the **Check** button. You will see a detailed description about the support duration:

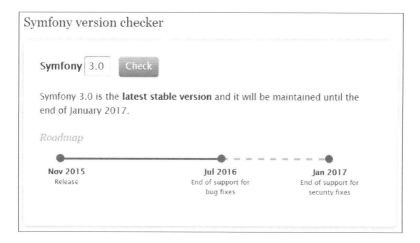

Checking the installation

To make sure that Symfony installed properly, first run the PHP built-in server:

```
$ bin/console server:run
```

Then, visit the following link in your browser:

```
http://localhost:8000/config.php
```

If you see the following image, then you are good to go. You can ignore the suggested recommendations for now:

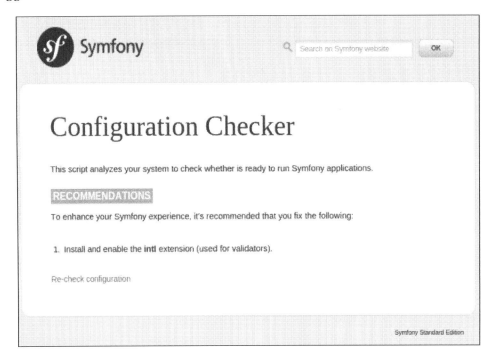

Summary

In this chapter, we read about the practicality of Symfony and the basic reasons why big companies are using it. We read about the Symfony road map and its potential. We ran the built-in web server to be able to see our Symfony instance. We saw how to use Composer to install Symfony and how to check the installation afterward.

In the next chapter, I will walk you through the request/response life cycle and show you how to use Symfony to generate code and shape it based on your needs.

2
The Request and Response Life Cycle

This chapter is a quick look at Symfony's fundamental features. We will use the request/response life cycle as a tool to discuss **Model-View-Controller** (**MVC**) in general and explore Symfony concepts such as routing, action (or controller, if you like), TWIG, Doctrine, and application setup. We will have a look at bundles and see how all of these concepts are organized in a bundle. Apart from creating a new bundle in this chapter, we will discuss the installation and how to modify and use bundles created by other developers.

The big picture

The request/response life cycle can be summarized in these two simple steps:

1. Firstly, you send your request by entering a URL in your browser.
2. The server then responds with a page and message (success, failure, and so on) depending on your request. End of story.

The following image shows an example of the request/response life cycle:

A web server receives a request and passes it to an action unit for further processing. In our case, this action unit is somewhere in Symfony and is in charge of receiving requests. Depending on their type, it will fetch a resource (such as a record from the database or an image from the server's hard drive) or do something (like sending an e-mail or assembling and returning a **JavaScript Object Notation (JSON)** string). Finally, it renders a page based on the results and sends it back to the browser. After the job is done, this action unit marks the request and response as terminated and looks for the next request, as shown in the following diagram:

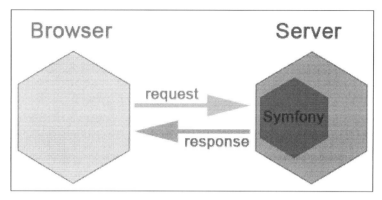

The general request/response life cycle on a server with Symfony

Look at your /web folder in your Symfony installation from the previous chapter. You can see that there is an app_dev.php file over there. Open the file (or the app. php file if you like) and pay attention to the last four lines:

```
$request = Request::createFromGlobals();
$response = $kernel->handle($request);
$response->send();
$kernel->terminate($request, $response);
```

These lines summarize the preceding story beautifully.

You can see how it is represented in the following screenshot. These are the four steps that Symfony takes to process a request and send a response:

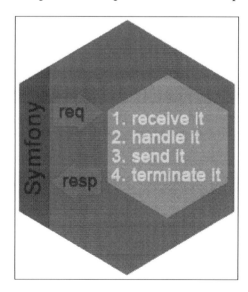

Well, that's the purpose of using Symfony. It sits on the web server and makes it serve for each receiving request. The second line calls a `handle()` method. This method is the main reason why we are here. It might look like just one innocent method, but in fact, the `handle()` method is in charge of managing other units that deal with databases, JSON strings, REST and SOAP requests, processing e-mails, rendering templates, and who knows what else in the future. Note that the `handle()` method manages the incoming requests by finding (routing) the right controller action and getting a response from it. However, it doesn't personally do the job itself. So do not underestimate the method. It might not look like doing much, but it controls everything. It makes the server components dance on the arrival of every single request.

Let's put this information in our big picture and see how it looks:

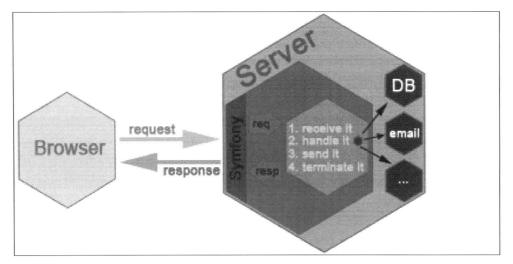

The handle() method facilitates the flow between the browser and server

Now we have a good template to refer to. In each of the following topics, I will update this big picture so that you can get the idea of each concept easily.

Anatomy of a bundle

When you install Symfony (via the default installer), it comes with a very basic controller and template. That is why we can see the default **Welcome!** screen by visiting the following URL:

```
http://localhost:8000
```

The general folder structure for a Symfony project is as follows:

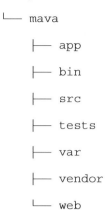

```
└── mava
    ├── app
    ├── bin
    ├── src
    ├── tests
    ├── var
    ├── vendor
    └── web
```

The folders that we are interested at the moment are `src/` and `app/`. They contain the code and template for the **Welcome!** screen. In the `src/` folder, we have a bundle called `AppBundle` with the following basic structure:

```
src/
└── AppBundle
    ├── AppBundle.php
    └── Controller
        └── DefaultController.php
```

The default controller is where the so-called `handle()` method passes the request and expects a response. Let's have a look in this controller:

```php
// mava/src/AppBundle/Controller/DefaultController.php
class DefaultController extends Controller
{
  /**
   * @Route("/", name="homepage")
   */
  public function indexAction(Request $request)
  {
    return $this->render('default/index.html.twig', [
      'base_dir' => realpath($this->container->
        getParameter('kernel.root_dir').'/..'),
    ]);
  }
}
```

Behind the scene, the `handle()` method asks the router to find a matching route for the home page request. The router looks at the available routes stack, finds the one defined for the `indexAction()` method, and passes the request to it.

If you are wondering what the route for `indexAction()` is, look at the `@Route()` annotation in the comments before the method body. This annotation defines the route for the action. You can prove it by looking at the available routes in the command line:

```
$ bin/console debug:router
```

Name	Method	Scheme	Host	Path
_wdt	ANY	ANY	ANY	/_wdt/{token}
_profiler_home	ANY	ANY	ANY	/_profiler/
...				
homepage	ANY	ANY	ANY	/

As you can see, the last line shows the route name and path for the home page.

Let's go back to controller `indexAction()` and see what happens to the request that we just received. We have only one simple `render()` function, which basically assembles a string for the project base URL and passes it to a template stored in the `Resources/` directory to be rendered.

The template engine gets the `base_dir` parameter, uses it in the available template, generates an HTML page, and returns it as the response.

This default bundle is minimized to the very basic structure and is for demonstration purposes only. Let's create a new bundle and see how it looks.

Generating a new bundle

There are two ways to create a new bundle. You can do it manually by creating classes or YAML files and organizing them in folders created manually in the `src/` folder of your project (and use your IDE's code generation feature to fill the blanks along the way).

You can also use the Symfony's interactive console to do the job for you. While you are at the root of the project, create a new bundle called `MyBundle` via the following command:

```
$ bin/console generate:bundle
```

Set the name and accept all default answers for the next questions. At the end, you will see a message confirming that the bundle was generated successfully:

```
> Generating a sample bundle skeleton into src/MyBundle OK!
> Checking that the bundle is autoloaded: OK
> Enabling the bundle inside app/AppKernel.php: OK
> Importing the bundle's routes from the app/config/routing.yml file: OK
> Importing the bundle's services.yml from the app/config/config.yml
file: OK
```

Let's see what each of these lines mean. The first line confirms that we have the folder structure for the new bundle. Check the `src/` directory and you will see this here:

```
src/
├── AppBundle
│   ├── AppBundle.php
│   └── Controller
│       └── DefaultController.php
└── MyBundle
    ├── Controller
    │   └── DefaultController.php
    ├── MyBundle.php
    ├── Resources
    │   ├── config
    │   │   └── services.yml
    │   └── views
    │       └── Default
    │           └── index.html.twig
    └── Tests
        └── Controller
            └── DefaultControllerTest.php
```

Compared to the default `AppBundle`, we have a few more files and folders in the generated bundle. We will get to that in a minute.

Now check the `AppKernel.php` file and, as you can see, the bundle is registered in our project:

```
// mava/app/AppKernel.php
class AppKernel extends Kernel
{
  public function registerBundles()
  {
    $bundles = [
      // . . .
      new AppBundle\AppBundle(),
      new MyBundle\MyBundle(),
    ];
  }
  // . . .
}
```

In the `app/config/routing.yml` file, we can see settings for the new bundle. We chose the default option while generating the bundle. This means that routes will be created from the controller action methods and their `@Route()` annotations:

```
# app/config/routing.yml
my:
  resource: "@MyBundle/Controller/"
  type:      annotation
  prefix:    /
```

Finally, in `app/config/config.yml`, the (future) services of our generated bundle are imported:

```
# app/config/config.yml
imports:
  - { resource: parameters.yml }
  - { resource: security.yml }
  - { resource: services.yml }
  - { resource: "@MyBundle/Resources/config/services.yml" }
```

This means that we are all set and good to start coding. To prove this, open the `DefaultController` for our new bundle and change `@Route()` as follows:

```
class DefaultController extends Controller
{
  /**
```

```
 * @Route("/my", name="mypage")
 */
public function indexAction()
{
  return $this->render('MyBundle:Default:index.html.twig');
}
}
```

Now, we can find the new route with the `debug:router` console command and we can see it in action by visiting `http://localhost:8000/my` in the browser.

Best practices

The question here is why do we need a new bundle? Couldn't we modify the current `AppBundle` instead? Yes, we could. Actually, it is totally up to you how you organize your code. Symfony won't complain about creating a new folder at the route of your project, naming it whatever you like, and organizing your code in a couple of subfolders over there. As long as you register your bundle in `AppKernel.php` and update the routing and config file with proper references, everything is fine.

Before doing this, ask yourself: does this contribute to the easier maintenance of your project? Think about the developers who are going to take over and maintain the code after you. We can have one bundle, call it `AppBundle`, and put all the application logic in its folders, or we can have as many bundles as we wish and create each piece of application logic in one of them (`UserBundle`, `ProjectBundle`, `TaskBundle`, and so on).

There is absolutely no right or wrong way and the way you organize your code has no effect on Symfony's performance. However, what I've learned from my past experiences is to keep things as simple as possible. Basically, from Symfony 3.x onward, I have decided to use the default Symfony application structure and `AppBundle` as a base for everything.

I create a new structure only if I need to reuse my code in some other projects (that is, a third-party bundle) or my project requires some specific configurations that cannot be met by default Symfony settings.

To help you make decisions about what to do and how to write and organize your code, Symfony has a best practices document that you can find here:

`http://symfony.com/doc/current/best_practices/index.html`

What I will do during this book is mention the related best practices for each topic in an information box where we need to make a decision about coding or organizing style.

To keep things simple and increase the project maintainability, keep your code in the `AppBundle`.

Custom bundles versus AppBundle

When we use `AppBundle` as a code base, the `app/` directory of our project can be seen as part of `AppBundle`. Sure, it has other files and folders that take care of other bundles available in the `/vendor` directory, for example, but we can benefit a lot from the `app/` folder.

For example, if you look at the `MyBundle/Resources` folder, you will find two subfolders named `Resources/config/` and `Resources/views/`, which hold service definitions (and other required settings in the future) and template files for that bundle.

However, with `AppBundle`, we already have a folder named `app/`, so conveniently, we can use the available `app/config` for our configuration needs and `app/Resources/views` for our templates. Using this approach, referencing these files are much easier.

Compare the `render()` method in `indexAction()` of each controller. In the `AppBundle` controller, we simply referenced the template file without mentioning the name of the bundle. When there is no bundle name, Symfony by default looks in the `app/Resources/views` directory to find the required template:

```
return $this->render('default/index.html.twig');
```

To check the contents of the `app/Resources/views` directory use the following command:

```
$ tree app/Resources/views/
app/Resources/views/
├── base.html.twig
└── default
    └── index.html.twig
```

In `MyBundle`, we have to mention the bundle name in the reference:

```
return $this->render('MyBundle:Default:index.html.twig');
```

Did you notice the `tests/` folder that Symfony created in the root of the project? We can use it to write tests for `AppBundle`.

We got two elements of MVC so far: Controller and View. Let's have a look at the big picture that we have now:

Creating templates with TWIG

Symfony has its own template engine called **TWIG**. It is a simple scripting language with a few tags and only three main rules:

- Whatever goes between {% %} should be executed
- Whatever is expressed via {{ }} should be printed
- Whatever is enclosed by {# #} is just a comment

As we continue, we will see how to use TWIG to create sophisticated and dynamic templates based on our project needs. For now, let's just see what a TWIG file looks like.

The `render()` method from the previous topic has two parameters: the path to our TWIG template and its parameter. By default, all templates are in the `app/Resources/views` folder. If you go there, you will find another folder called `default`. That's why the middle part of the path parameter is `default`:

```
return $this->render('default/index.html.twig', [
    'base_dir' => realpath($this->container-
        >getParameter('kernel.root_dir').'/..'),
]);
```

Obviously, in the `default` folder, we have the template file itself. So basically, we follow the `[subdirectory in /Resources/views]/[template name]` format to access our templates.

There are two questions here:

- Why didn't we mention the full path as `Resources/views/Default`?

  By default, Symfony knows that all templates should be organized in `Resources/views`, so we can ignore that part and keep references nice and short.

- Why do we even need a subfolder in `Resources/views`? Wouldn't it be cleaner and shorter if we keep every template in the root of `Resources/views`?

  Yes, you can, but it is not very well organized. For example, imagine that we have several routes for different menu items: `/about`, `/about/{name}` and `/project`, `/project/{id}`. You can keep templates for these routes in the root and give them unique names, or you can create subfolders `About/` and `Project/` and keep the related templates in each of them.

Controller/View interaction

Let's add a new controller action in `AppBundle` and call it `aboutAction()`. This method will receive a name and says something about it:

```
// mava/src/AppBundle/Controller/DefaultController.php
class DefaultController extends Controller
{
// ...
  /**
   * @Route("/about/{name}", name="aboutpage")
   */
  public function aboutAction($name)
  {
    return $this->render('about/index.html.twig', array('name' =>
      $name));
  }
}
```

The new `@Route()` annotation for this method suggests that we need a new folder called `about/` and an index template as follows:

```
{# mava/app/Resources/views/About/index.html.twig #}
Hello {{ name|capitalize }}! <br/>
Today is: {{"now"|date("m/d/Y")}}
```

As you can see, we can decorate the contents of a .twig file in any way you like. For example, we can capitalize the name using the capitalize filter and show the date by applying the date() filter to the current timestamp.

 There is a lot to say about TWIG and I will show you how to use it practically in the chapters to come.

User is one of the key entities of our project. They will be recognized as team members and organized in several different groups. Keeping this in mind, let's create an **about** page and see how we can see details about a specific user.

Conditional templates

In the previous example, imagine that we want to make the {name} parameters optional. In other words, if there is a name in the URL, then we want to see a name-related message, and if there is no name, then we want to see a general message.

Let's start by changing the @Route() annotation:

```
// mava/src/AppBundle/Controller/DefaultController.php
class DefaultController extends Controller
{
  // . . .
  /**
   * @Route("/about/{name}", name="aboutpage",
       defaults={"name":null})
   */
  public function aboutAction($name)
  {
    return $this->render('about/index.html.twig', array('name' =>
      $name));
  }
}
```

The defaults parameter nominates a default value for the name variable. If we don't set a value for name, then it will be set to null. So now our aboutAction() can receive requests from both /about and about/{name}.

Let's see how the template can handle these requests. Get rid of the previous contents of `About/index.html.twig` and replace them with the following blocks:

```
{# mava/app/Resources/views/About/index.html.twig #}
{% if name %}
  {{name}} is a member of our team.
{% else %}
  mava is a web app for task management and team collaboration. <br/>
{% endif %}
```

As you noticed, I used the `{% if <condition> %}` tag to create a conditional structure. The idea is to create one template to handle various routes. Sure, we could create two separate templates and routes for `/about` and `/about/name`, but that's how we can work smarter and not harder. So basically, our template says that if I see a value for the `name` variable, I will go in the `if` block; otherwise, I will follow the `else` block.

Make it dynamic

So far, it was about a static controller dealing with a static template. Let's see how we can feed our template with data from a database. Instead of handling database queries directly, we will use an **Object Relational Mapper (ORM)**.

 Doctrine is the ORM that we are using in this book. It is powerful and by default integrated into Symfony, which makes it very convenient to use.

The Doctrine's job is to treat PHP classes and objects like they are tables and records. This way, we don't need to write SQL queries for **Create**, **Read**, **Update**, and **Delete** (**CRUD**) actions. All we need to do is ask our ORM to do the job for us. That makes coding a lot easier and fun.

Database configurations

Before using Doctrine, we need to make sure that our database settings are correct. Make sure that you have installed MySQL and its PHP drivers already and you have a valid MySQL username and password. You might find database management applications handy. I use MySQL Workbench, but feel free to choose anything that appeals to you.

To check the database configuration in your Symfony project, open the `app/config/parameters.yml` file and set your own db username and password:

```
# app/config/parameters.yml
parameters:
  database_driver: pdo_mysql
  database_host: 127.0.0.1
  database_port: null
  database_name: mava
  database_user: <Your Username>
  database_password: <Your Password>
  mailer_transport: smtp
  mailer_host: 127.0.0.1
  mailer_user: null
  mailer_password: null
  locale: en
  secret: ThisTokenIsNotSoSecretChangeIt
  debug_toolbar: true
  debug_redirects: false
  use_assetic_controller: true
```

As you can see, the database name for our project is `mava`. To create this database, run the following command:

```
$ bin/console doctrine:database:create
```

Generating an entity

The database is created and we can create our tables in it. In Doctrine terminology, we don't call them tables anymore. Technically, they are PHP classes called entities. To generate an entity named `User`, run the following command:

```
$ bin/console doctrine:generate:entity
```

Then, follow the interactive steps as follows:

```
The Entity shortcut name: AppBundle:User
Determine the format to use for the mapping information.
Configuration format (yml, xml, php, or annotation) [annotation]:
```

We only need three fields for our entity:

```
New field name (press <return> to stop adding fields): name
Field type [string]:
Field length [255]:
```

```
Is nullable [false]:
Unique [false]:


New field name (press <return> to stop adding fields): bio
Field type [string]: text
Is nullable [false]:
Unique [false]:


New field name (press <return> to stop adding fields): email
Field type [string]:
Field length [255]:
Is nullable [false]:
Unique [false]:
```

If you check your database, you won't see the new table yet but there are some changes in our bundle directory.

There is a new Entity/ folder in our bundle and a PHP class called User.php in it. This file contains some property definitions and getter and setter methods for each property:

```php
/**
 * @var string
 * @ORM\Column(name="name", type="string", length=255)
 */
private $name;

/**
 * Set name
 * @param string $name
 * @return User
 */
public function setName($name)
{
  $this->name = $name;
  return $this;
}

/**
 * Get name
 * @return string
 */
```

```
public function getName()
{
    return $this->name;
}
```

The comments before the variable and method definition are not just ordinary comments. They are generated by console (when we choose an annotation) and a way of communication between our entity and Doctrine. For example, take a look at this comment:

```
/**
 * @var string
 * @ORM\Column(name="name", type="string", length=255)
 */
```

It tells Doctrine that we need a column called `name` with a `string` (255) type. Now that we have our entity defined, it is time to generate the related table in our database:

```
$ bin/console doctrine:schema:update --force
```

Check your database now and you will see the `User` table over there. For more details about the Doctrine annotation, visit `http://docs.doctrine-project.org/projects/doctrine-orm/en/latest/reference/annotations-reference.html`.

Installing bundles created by others

To play with our new entity, we need some records. We can add records manually or we can ask Symfony's console to do the job for us. These sample records are called data fixtures and there is a bundle to load and use fixtures. This bundle is called `doctrine-fixtures-bundle` and this is how we install it:

1. In the root of your project open `composer.json` file and add the following entry to it:

    ```
    "require": {
      //...
      "doctrine/doctrine-fixtures-bundle": "2.3.0"
    },
    ```

2. Now add this bundle to your `vendor/` folder:

    ```
    $ composer update doctrine/doctrine-fixtures-bundle
    ```

3. Finally, open the `app/AppKernel.php` file and add the following line at the end of the `$bundles` array:

```
// app/AppKernel.php
//...
$bundles = array(
  //...
  new Doctrine\Bundle\FixturesBundle\DoctrineFixturesBundle(),
  );
//...
```

Congratulations, you just installed a new bundle in your project! To load data fixtures in our entity, we need to create them first.

Creating data fixtures

Technically, a data fixture is a PHP class with a few initialized objects. In `AppBundle`, create this directory and file structure:

`/DataFixtures/ORM/LoadUsers.php`

Add the following content to our class:

```php
<?php
// mava/src/AppBundle/DataFixtures/ORM/LoadUsers.php
namespace AppBundle\DataFixtures\ORM;
use Doctrine\Common\DataFixtures\FixtureInterface;
use Doctrine\Common\Persistence\ObjectManager;
use AppBundle\Entity\User;

class LoadUsers implements FixtureInterface
{
  public function load(ObjectManager $manager)
  {
    // todo: create and persist objects
  }
}
```

This is the general structure of a data fixture. As you can see, it implements `FixtureInterface` and has a `load()` method for data persistence.

All we need to do is create a few objects, set their values, and ask our object manager to persist them:

```
public function load(ObjectManager $manager)
{
  $user1 = new User();
  $user1->setName('John');
  $user1->setBio('He is a cool guy');
  $user1->setEmail('john@mava.info');
  $manager->persist($user1);

  $user2 = new User();
  $user2->setName('Jack');
  $user2->setBio('He is a cool guy too');
  $user2->setEmail('jack@mava.info');
  $manager->persist($user2);

  $manager->flush();
}
```

Remember those setters and getters in our User entity? That's how we use them here. These two objects are all set and ready to be persisted in our database. The flush() method executes both queries in one shot. This means that we can have multiple queries created and run them in one step. This is the beauty of Doctrine. Now we are all set and ready to load what we have created.

Loading data fixtures

Loading can be done via a simple command:

```
$ bin/console doctrine:fixtures:load
```

It will ask you if you want to erase the previous content of the table first. Answer *Y* and press *Enter*:

```
Careful, database will be purged. Do you want to continue Y/N ?Y
  > purging database
  > loading mava\CoreBundle\DataFixtures\ORM\LoadUsers
```

Now check your `User` table. As you can see, there are two new records here:

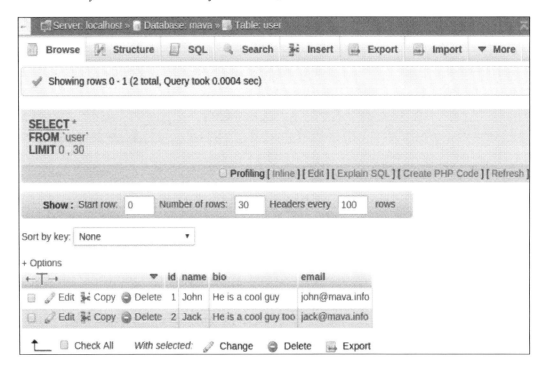

 In case you decide to append new records to the current table, use the following command:

```
$ bin/console doctrine:fixtures:load --append
```

Dynamic templates and controllers

Now that we have a few records in our table, let's see how to fetch them via controller and feed their properties to our templates. What we expect from our dynamic template is to receive an object and show its properties. In our case, the object is `User` and its properties are `name`, `bio`, and `email`. So, edit the `about/index.html.twig` template as follows:

```
{# mava/app/Resources/views/about/index.html.twig #}

{% if user %}
  <h1>User Profile</h1>
  <strong>Name: </strong>{{user.name}} <br/>
```

```
<strong>email: </strong>{{user.email}} <br/>
<strong>Bio: </strong>{{user.bio}} <br/>
{% else %}
  mava is a web app for task management and team collaboration. <br/>
{% endif %}
```

Next, add a few lines to `aboutAction()` to retrieve information about the given user:

```php
<?php
// AppBundle/Controller/DefaultController.php
// ...
use AppBundle\Entity\User;
// ...
  /**
   * @Route("/about/{name}", name="aboutpage",
     defaults={"name":null})
   */
  public function aboutAction($name)
  {
    if ($name) {
      $user = $this->getDoctrine()
      ->getRepository('AppBundle:User')
      ->findOneBy(array('name'=>$name));
      if (false === $user instanceof User) {
        throw $this->createNotFoundException(
          'No user named '.$name.' found!'
        );
      }
    }
    return $this->render('about/index.html.twig', array('user' =>
      $user));
  }
```

This action first accesses the Doctrine service, and, via this, approaches the `User` entity. The next step would be to find the first record that has a `john` value for its `name` property.

If no record is found, an exception will be thrown; otherwise, the found object will be passed to the `index.html.twig` template.

That's it. If you visit the `http://localhost:8000/about/john` or
`http://localhost:8000/about/jack` URL, you will see that it works as we expected:

The big picture with MVC

We have already seen how the controller and view parts of MVC fit into the request/
response life cycle. In every project, the database is the place to keep the business
logic; this is why it is called model. In the model part of MVC, we define entities and
the relationship between them. In our example, the `User` entity is part of our model.

The big picture can be updated as follows:

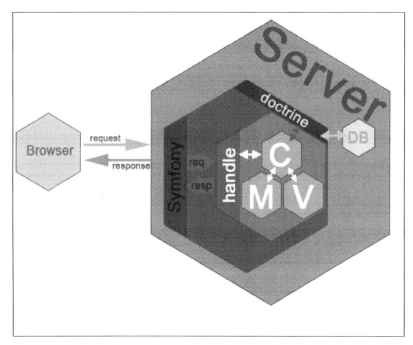

Symfony MVC interactions in a request/response life cycle

Summary

In this chapter, we were provided with a bird's-eye view of the request/response life cycle. You learned how Symfony deals with requests and how Model, View, and Controller fit into this image.

We saw how to use a console to generate loads of useful classes and set up dynamic templates, routes, and controllers. Finally, we saw how to harness the power of Doctrine to deal with database-related requests.

As I mentioned at the beginning, this was a quick look at Symfony's popular features to warm you up for what is coming next.

In the next two chapters, there won't be any development. Instead, we will have a lot of environment settings to make sure that our development process goes as smoothly as possible.

3
Setting Up the Environment

This chapter might give you the impression of doing a system administrator's job. It is all about setting up a few accounts and configuring functionality for **Continuous Integration** (CI).

First, we will take a look at the definition of CI and understand why it is not a *luxury* anymore, rather, a *must have* feature in any project. Then, we will see how to utilize Amazon Web Services to set up a test and deployment server.

We will use Jenkins as a CI application and show you how to integrate it into your Amazon Web Services account, install required plugins to test PHP projects, and finally, prepare our Symfony project to benefit from the whole infrastructure.

When everything is set up properly, we will create a simple testing code and watch how CI does the rest of the jobs: running tests, generating reports, and deploying the application automatically.

As you may have guessed, we won't have much Symfony development in this chapter. However, once CI is in place, we will see how easy, elegant, and professional the rest of our journey will be.

In this chapter, we will cover the following topics:

- Discussing the importance of Continuous Integration
- Using Amazon Web Services
- Using Elastic Compute Cloud
- Setting up the server
- Setting up Simple Email Service
- Installing PHP tools
- Orchestrating the build process
- Creating a new job in Jenkins
- Running the first build

The importance of Continuous Integration

Imagine that we are a team working on the subject of this book (which is a task management and team collaboration web application). Suppose that I'm working on `CoreBundle`, you are working on `ProjectBundle`, and James (another developer) is working on `UserBundle`. As individuals, we are doing our job professionally; we create tests and scenarios, maintain best practices for the coding, and make sure that all tests pass successfully every time we finish developing a new feature. However, there is one big problem here. There is not that much communication here because we work individually.

Having said this, we will much likely experience *Integration Hell* at the end when we try to integrate all the individual components into the main application. Statistics show that the amount of resources spent on fixing these integration issues sometimes equals to the same amount spent on creating the code itself.

CI is a software development practice that helps catch integration bugs the moment they are born. It is like a big brother watching every member of the development team and, as soon as he/she tries to integrate a new feature into the main application, big brother takes the code, runs everyone's tests against it, generates some reports, and only if everything is okay, generates a fresh build for the project and notifies everyone about it.

The moral of the story is it does not make bugs disappear, but because it looks for them constantly, finding and fixing them is easier and faster.

Amazon Web Services

Our digital assets are mostly on the cloud these days. Think about where you keep photos, music, blogs, and documents. Sure, you might have a local backup, but most of us have an account and access our digital assets via a website.

Amazon Web Services (**AWS**) is a cloud computing platform. It contains several building blocks that offer flexibility to create almost any cloud service you can dream about, from hosting digital assets mentioned in the previous paragraph to a **Software as a Service** (**SaaS**) web application, which is the purpose of this book. The good news is that you don't need to pay for this and, thanks to Amazon's generosity, there is a one-year free tier membership. Simply visit `https://aws.amazon.com/free/` and click on the **Create a Free Account** button, as shown in the following screenshot:

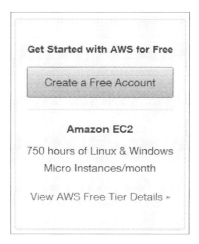

In this chapter, we are going to use two AWS for our project: EC2 and SES. To find out what these abbreviations stand for and what they do, keep reading.

To give you an idea of how we are going to use AWS, the overall architectural diagram of our project will be something as follows:

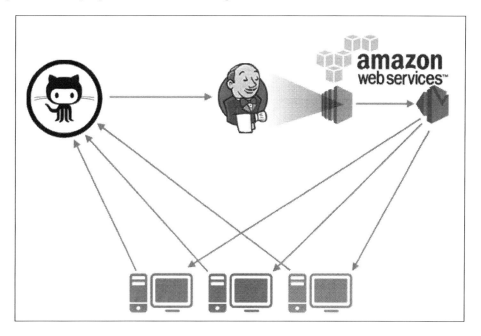

First, developers push their changes to the GitHub repository. Then, Jenkins, which is installed in our CI server, pulls these changes and runs tests, generates reports, and makes a new build automatically. Finally, a notification e-mail is sent via SES to the team.

Yes, we are going to use Jenkins as our CI application. It is robust, easy to install, and comes with loads of out-of-the-box features that we can use. To install Jenkins, we need to set up our CI server first.

Elastic Compute Cloud

Amazon **Elastic Compute Cloud (EC2)** is the largest public cloud in the world and we will use EC2 to set up our CI server.

Assuming that you have already created your free account on AWS, you should be able to see the console area when you log in.

As you can see in the following image, it is packed with loads of components, and if this is the first time you are here, it might look overwhelming. Don't worry, we only need two of these services for this chapter:

Creating a new instance

Our CI server is basically a virtual machine running Linux, which, in AWS terminology, is called an **instance**. So, from now on, when you see the term instance, it means a virtual machine on the cloud. To create your first instance, follow these steps:

1. Under the **Compute & Networking** option, click on **EC2**.

2. Before doing anything, you need to select the right region for better performance. In the upper-right hand corner of the page, there is a drop-down list where you can select the closest area to you, as shown in the following screenshot:

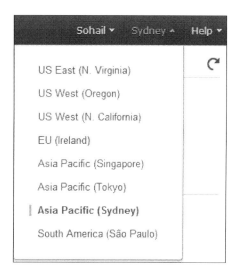

3. Now, click on the big blue button saying **Launch Instance** and select the latest version of the Ubuntu server. Pay attention; some options have a **Free tier eligible** label and some don't. After selecting EC2, a validation from Amazon is required. This validation could take from several minutes to days:

4. As you can see in the following screenshot, only **t2.micro** is free. Select this plan and click on **Next: Configure Instance Details**.

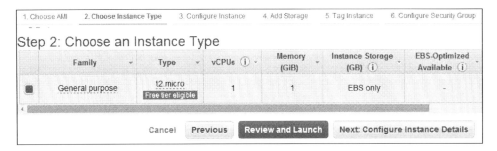

5. The next two steps are configuration (**3. Configure Instance**) and adding storage (**4. Add Storage**). Simply accept the default settings and move on to **Step 5: Tag Instance**. Here, we will choose a Tag name for our virtual machine. Enter the name `Mava` in the **Value** field and proceed to the next step:

6. This step is where you set up the firewall for your CI server and define which ports should be open to the outside world. In the **Security group name** field, type `Mava`. We need SSH and HTTP access to our server, so click on the **Add Rule** button, choose **HTTP**, and press the **Review and Launch** button:

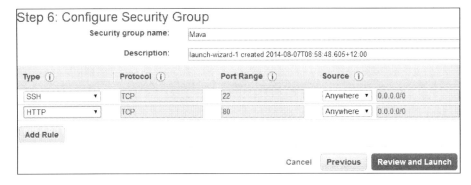

7. When you press the **Review and Launch** button, as shown in the following screenshot, it asks for a public and private key pair in order to access our EC2 instance. Choose **Create a new key pair**. Type the name `mava-keys` for it. Now you can click on the **Launch Instances** button. It takes a few seconds to generate the instance and when it is finished, you can click on the **View Instances** button to see it. Be patient as it takes a while to change the status from pending to running:

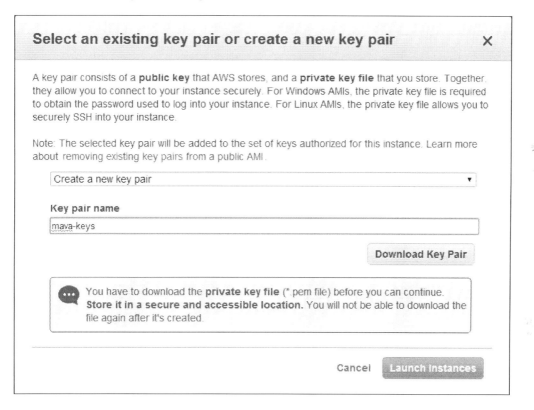

 Do not lose your key. If you lose it, you have to delete your instance completely and start over again. Due to security reasons, Amazon doesn't keep a backup of your key.

8. While it is in the running mode, click on your instance and copy the **Public DNS** address:

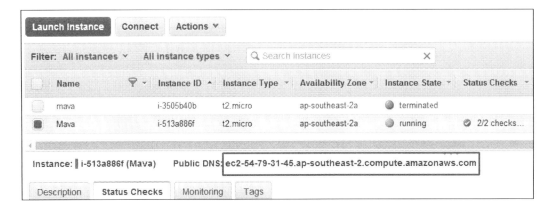

9. Right now, you have enough information to connect to your EC2 instance:

    ```
    ssh -i ~/Downloads/mava-keys.pem ubuntu@ec2-54-79-31-45.ap-
    southeast-2.compute.amazonaws.com
    ```

    However, this is a very long command and not very safe as well. First, we want to make sure that only we have read and write access to our key. So fire a terminal window, copy the instance key to your `.ssh` folder, and set the permission as follows:

    ```
    $ mv ~/Downloads/mava-keys.pem ~/.ssh/
    ```

    ```
    $ chmod 400 ~/.ssh/mava-keys.pem
    ```

10. Now, for more convenience, let's create an alias for that long `ssh` command. Open the `.ssh/config` file and add the following contents to it. Remember that for `Hostname`, you have to add your own Public DNS value that you copied from step 8:

    ```
    Host ec2
       Hostname ec2-54-79-31-45.ap-southeast-
         2.compute.amazonaws.com
       User          ubuntu
       IdentityFile  ~/.ssh/mava-keys.pem
    ```

11. Now you can connect to your instance via this short command:

    ```
    ssh ec2
    ```

12. For the first time, you will be prompted with the following:

    ```
    Are you sure you want to continue connecting (yes/no)? Yes
    ```

13. Answer `Yes` and congratulations! You are now connected to your EC2 instance on the Amazon cloud:

```
ubuntu@ip-172-31-29-153:~$
```

Setting up the server

Now that we have our instance set up and we are connected to it successfully, it is time to add the required tools and components to it. Basically, it is a fresh Ubuntu box with nothing on it. To make it act like a CI server, we need to install **LAMP** (**Linux**, **Apache**, **MySQL**, and **PHP**), **Jenkins**, and a few other libraries.

Installing Apache

Having the Linux in place already, let's start by installing the Apache web server:

1. Before installing anything, first of all, update your Linux packages and install English language packs and locales:

   ```
   $ sudo apt-get update
   ```

2. Then, install the locale package as follows:

   ```
   $ sudo apt-get install language-pack-en
   ```

3. Now we can install Apache2 and some required modules to proxy the Jenkins server:

   ```
   $ sudo apt-get install apache2
   $ sudo a2enmod proxy
   $ sudo a2enmod proxy_http
   ```

4. Now restart Apache:

   ```
   $ sudo service apache2 restart
   ```

Apache2 is now installed and ready to serve web requests.

Installing MySQL and PHP

To finalize the LAMP stack, we need to install MySQL and PHP:

```
$ sudo apt-get install php5 php5-mysql mysql-client mysql-server
```

Enter your MySQL password for the root user when you are prompted.

Installing Jenkins

Installing Jenkins is a three-step process:

1. First, we need to add the Jenkins package to our Linux repositories and update them:

   ```
   $ wget -q -O - http://pkg.jenkins-ci.org/debian/jenkins-ci.org.key
   | sudo apt-key add -
   $ echo "deb http://pkg.jenkins-ci.org/debian binary/" | sudo tee
   -a /etc/apt/sources.list.d/jenkins.list
   $ sudo apt-get update
   ```

2. Then, we need to install Jenkins:

   ```
   $ sudo apt-get install jenkins
   ```

3. Finally, we need to set up a virtual host for our Jenkins application. To do so, create a new `jenkins.conf` file and add the following content to it:

   ```
   $ sudo vim /etc/apache2/sites-available/jenkins.conf

   <VirtualHost *:80>
     ServerName ec2-54-79-31-45.ap-southeast-2.compute.amazonaws.com
     ProxyRequests Off
     <Proxy *>
         Order deny,allow
         Allow from all
     </Proxy>
     ProxyPreserveHost on
     ProxyPass / http://localhost:8080/
   </VirtualHost>
   ```

4. Now enable the site:

   ```
   $ sudo a2ensite jenkins
   ```

5. Restart Apache:

   ```
   $ sudo apache2 reload
   ```

To test your installation, simply fire a browser window and visit your hostname (in my case, ec2-54-79-31-45.ap-southeast-2.compute.amazonaws.com). If everything is set up properly, you should be able to see a welcome page as follows:

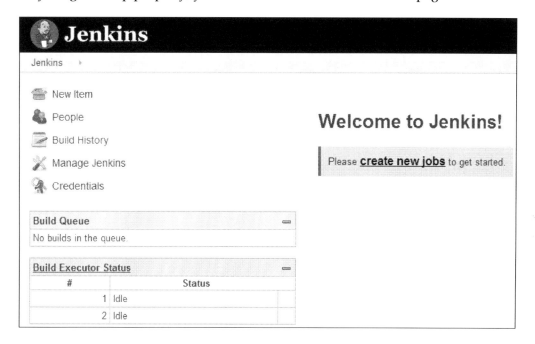

So far, we set up a free AWS account, created an EC2 instance (a Ubuntu virtual machine), and installed a LAMP stack and Jenkins in it. Now we are ready to configure Jenkins.

Setting up security and installing plugins in Jenkins

We need some sort of security to make sure that only an authorized user can access and manage Jenkins:

1. First, we need to set the security. Navigate to **Manage Jenkins | Configure Global Security** and check the **Enable security** box:

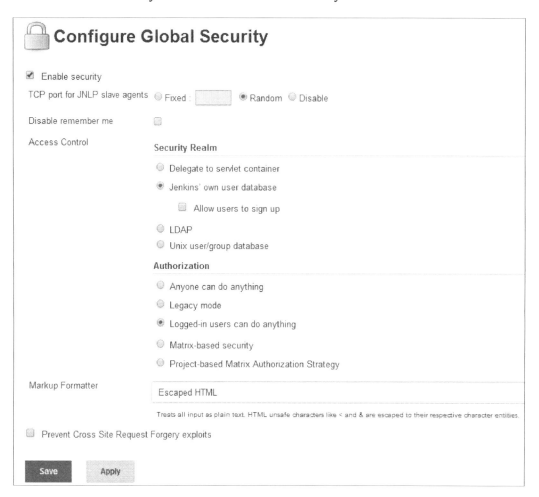

Note that the options you choose for your security are totally dependent on your projects and needs. For this book, select the options that you see in the preceding image.

2. As soon as you press the **Save** button, you will be asked for a username and password. Simply click on the **Jenkins** link on top of the page to lead to a sign-up page. Fill in the form here and press **Sign up**:

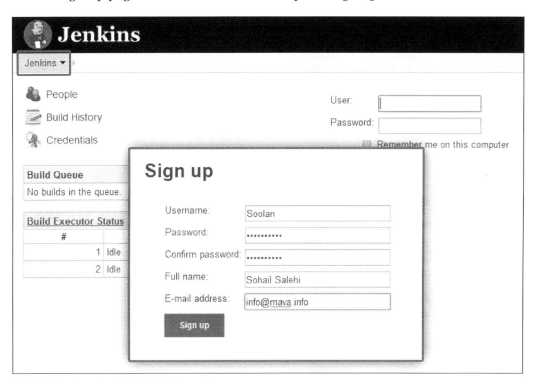

3. Now, we need to install plugins required for CI. Navigate to **Manage Jenkins | Manage Plug-ins**, and you will see that there are some plugins installed already in the **Updates** tab. Before installing any new plugins, select them all and update them:

Jenkins › Plugin Manager			

Updates	Available	Installed	Advanced

Install	Name ↓	Version	Installed
☑	**Credentials Plugin** This plugin allows you to store credentials in Jenkins.	1.15	1.9.4
☑	**CVS Plugin** This bundled plugin integrates Jenkins with CVS version control system.	2.12	2.11
☑	**Javadoc Plugin** This plugin adds Javadoc support to Jenkins.	1.2	1.1
☑	**LDAP Plugin** Security realm based on LDAP authentication. Warning: the new version of this plugin claims to use a different settings format than the installed version. Jobs using this plugin may need to be reconfigured, and/or you may not be able to cleanly revert to the prior version without manually restoring old settings. Consult the plugin release notes for details.	1.10.2	1.6
☑	**Mailer** This plugin allows you to configure email notifications. This is a break-out of the	1.9	1.8

Download now and install after restart

4. When you press the **Download now and install after restart** button, a progress page shows up with the list of plugins to install. Check the option at the bottom of this page to restart Jenkins:

Installing Plugins/Upgrades

Preparation

- Checking internet connectivity
- Checking update center connectivity
- Success

OWASP Markup Formatter Plugin	Downloaded Successfully. Will be activated during the next boot
Translation Assistance Plugin	Downloaded Successfully. Will be activated during the next boot
LDAP Plugin	Downloaded Successfully. Will be activated during the next boot
CVS Plugin	Downloaded Successfully. Will be activated during the next boot
Mailer	Downloaded Successfully. Will be activated during the next boot
Matrix Authorization Strategy Plugin	Downloaded Successfully. Will be activated during the next boot
Matrix Project Plugin	Installing
Credentials Plugin	Pending
SSH Credentials Plugin	Pending
SSH Slaves plugin	Pending
MapDB API Plugin	Pending
SCM API Plugin	Pending
Subversion Plugin	Pending
SSH Credentials Plugin	Pending
Javadoc Plugin	Pending
Credentials Plugin	Pending
Restarting Jenkins	Pending

Go back to the top page
(you can start using the installed plugins right away)

☑ Restart Jenkins when installation is complete and no jobs are running

Note that when you restart Jenkins, it might take a couple of minutes and ask you to log in again.

5. Now, go to the **Manage Plug-in** page again and visit the **Available** tab this time. On the search field, look for the following plugins one by one, select them, and when they are all selected, download and install them. Each plugin should be self-explanatory, but if you want more details about each one of them, visit their websites and read the documentation:

   ○ GitHub (access to GitHub repositories)

   ○ Checkstyle (reading CodeSniffer logs in the Checkstyle format)

   ○ Clover PHP (processing PHPUnit's Clover log file)

   ○ Crap4J (processing PHPUnit's Crap4J XML log file)

   ○ DRY (processing phpcpd logs in the PMD-CPD format)

   ○ HTML Publisher (publishing documentation generated by phpDox, for instance)

   ○ JDepend (processing PHP_Depend logs in the JDepend format)

   ○ Plot (processing phploc CSV output)

   ○ PMD (processing PHPMD log files in the PMD format)

   ○ Violations (processing various log files)

   ○ xUnit (processing PHPUnit's JUnit XML log file)

6. Apart from adding the GitHub plugin to Jenkins, we need to go back to our instance terminal and install Git here:

   ```
   $ sudo apt-get install git
   ```

Now security settings and required plugins are in place and ready to set up management settings. Before that, we need to set up a mail server. This mail server will act as a notification system. In other words, every time a build is made successfully or fails or some reports are generated during CI, we need to be informed about it. So we need a mail server to send these notifications to us.

AWS comes with a service to handle e-mails, and we are about to see how to use it in our project.

Simple Email Service

Amazon **Simple Email Service (SES)** is an SMTP server to send limited amounts of e-mails per day. At the time of writing this book, it is about 200 e-mails per day, which is more than enough. To set up SES, follow these steps:

1. On the console page, click on **SES** under **App Services**:

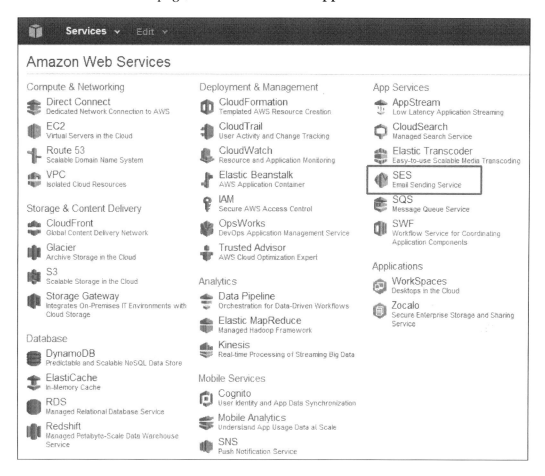

2. On the next page, click on **SMTP Settings**, and copy the server name and port number to a file as you will need them for the next step:

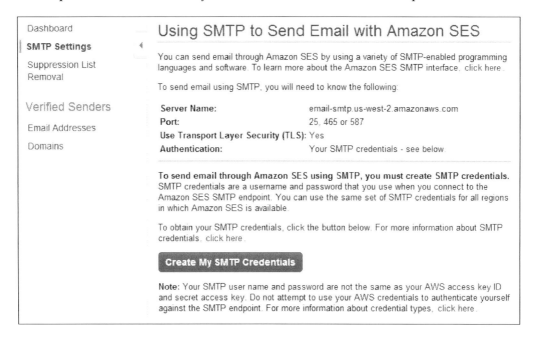

3. Click on the **Create My SMTP Credentials** button and wait until you are redirected to the IAM service (another Amazon service to manage credentials). Click on the **Create** button:

4. Copy and paste the username and password fields in the following page because you will need them for the next topic as well:

 The credentials provided here are fake. Don't use them. Use your custom ones. You don't think I'm going to expose my password to the world, do you?

Configuring Jenkins

Now that we have the mail server and Jenkins plugins in place, it is time to configure Jenkins itself, by preforming the following steps:

1. Navigate to **Manage Jenkins | Configure System** and, leaving all other settings as default, scroll down to **Jenkins Location**. As you can see, it is already set to our EC2 instance. Set the e-mail address that you want all notifications sent from:

2. Under **SSH Server**, disable **SSHD port**.

3. Scroll further down to the **E-mail Notification** section and click on the **Advanced** button. Check **Use SMTP Authentication** and **Use SSL**. Now fill in this form with SMTP server settings that you did from the previous section:

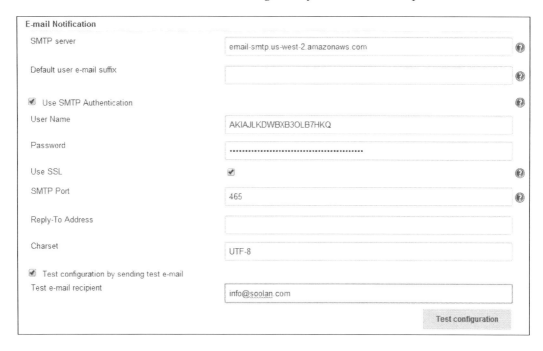

If you'd rather use your own SMTP settings instead of SES, feel free to replace this form with your settings.

4. Click on the **Test configuration** button, and if everything is set up correctly, you will see a success message and receive an e-mail shortly.

5. Finally, click on the **Save** button at the bottom of this page.

Installing PHP tools

We installed some plugins in our Jenkins, but to make these plugins work, we need to install some PHP tools on our EC2 instance. We can install these tools via Composer on our Symfony project, but this is not a good practice. They will sit in the vendor/ directory and make our Symfony project big and heavy.

Instead, we are going to install them in the CI server itself and benefit from them for every project we define in Jenkins:

1. Assuming that the SSH connection to our EC2 instance is still live, open a terminal window and add the following PEAR channels to the system:

```
$ sudo pear channel-discover pear.pdepend.org
```

```
$ sudo pear channel-discover pear.phpmd.org
```

```
$ sudo pear channel-discover pear.phpdoc.org
```

```
$ sudo pear channel-discover pear.symfony-project.com
```

2. Now install PHP tools as follows:

```
$ sudo pear install pdepend/PHP_Depend
```

```
$ sudo pear install phpmd/PHP_PMD
```

```
$ sudo pear install phpunit/phpcpd
```

```
$ sudo pear install phpunit/phploc
```

```
$ sudo pear install --alldeps phpunit/PHP_CodeBrowser
```

```
$ sudo pear install phpdoc/phpDocumentor-alpha
```

> You might have used some of these tools and some of them might look new to you. I am not going to go through all of them and explain what they do. It needs another book to go through all the details. Instead, I encourage you to have a look at their documentation and briefly familiarize yourself with their functions.
>
> You can find a list of URLs for these tools on their official website or https://packagist.org/.

One last thing that you may notice is why we didn't install these packages via Composer. Note the following command:

```
$ sudo pear install phpunit/phpcpd
```

It is better if you replace the preceding command with this one:

```
$ sudo composer global require 'sebastian/phpcpd=*'
```

It is certainly better to use Composer. However, there is a catch to this. I've noticed that when you install packages via Composer, for some reason Jenkins doesn't like it and fixing build bugs might give you a major headache. So, to play it safe, install them via PEAR channel and play with Jenkins for a while. When you master the basics, there is always room for creating more EC2 instances and setting up the required tools like a pro.

You can find more about the basics on the `http://jenkins.org/` website.

Sniff Symfony codes

Symfony has its own coding standards. To benefit from CodeSniffer in our project, we need to introduce Symfony standards and make it the default standard:

1. First, find the PEAR directory:

   ```
   $ pear config-show | grep php_dir
   ```

2. Now, go to the `Standards` folder in CodeSniffer (in our EC2 instance, the path is `cd /usr/share/php/PHP/CodeSniffer/Standards/`) and clone the following repository:

   ```
   $ sudo git clone git://github.com/escapestudios/Symfony2-coding-
   standard.git Symfony2
   ```

3. Now make Symfony the default coding standard:

   ```
   $ phpcs --config-set default_standard Symfony2
   ```

Orchestrating the build process

To automate the build process, we are going to use Apache Ant. Ant looks for a `build.xml` file in the root of the Symfony project, parses the contents, and based on what it finds, starts to run the PHP tools that we installed earlier.

So, in the root of your project, create the `build.xml` file with the following content (you can grab this file from the project's GitHub repository, `https://github.com/Soolan/mava-project`):

```xml
<?xml version="1.0" encoding="UTF-8"?>

<project name="Mava" default="build">
  <property name="workspace" value="${basedir}" />
  <property name="sourcedir" value="${basedir}/src" />
  <property name="builddir" value="${workspace}/app/build" />

  <target name="build"
```

```
      depends="prepare,vendors,parameters,lint,phploc,pdepend,
        phpcpd,phpmd-ci,phpcs-ci,phpdoc,phpunit,phpcb"/>

<target name="build-parallel" depends="prepare,lint,tools-
  parallel,phpunit,phpcb"/>

<target name="tools-parallel" description="Run tools in
  parallel">
  <parallel threadCount="2">
    <sequential>
      <antcall target="pdepend"/>
      <antcall target="phpmd-ci"/>
    </sequential>
    <antcall target="phpcpd"/>
    <antcall target="phpcs-ci"/>
    <antcall target="phploc"/>
    <antcall target="phpdoc"/>
  </parallel>
</target>

<target name="clean" description="Cleanup build artifacts">
  <delete dir="${builddir}/api"/>
  <delete dir="${builddir}/code-browser"/>
  <delete dir="${builddir}/coverage"/>
  <delete dir="${builddir}/logs"/>
  <delete dir="${builddir}/pdepend"/>
  <delete dir="${builddir}/docs/*"/>
</target>

<target name="prepare" depends="clean" description="Prepare for
  build">
  <mkdir dir="${builddir}/api"/>
  <mkdir dir="${builddir}/code-browser"/>
  <mkdir dir="${builddir}/coverage"/>
  <mkdir dir="${builddir}/logs"/>
  <mkdir dir="${builddir}/pdepend"/>
</target>

<target name="lint" description="Perform syntax check of
  sourcecode files">
  <apply executable="php" failonerror="true">
  <arg value="-l" />
  <fileset dir="${sourcedir}">
    <include name="**/*.php" />
    <modified />
```

```
    </fileset>
    <fileset dir="${basedir}/src/">
      <include name="**/*Test.php" />
      <modified />
    </fileset>
    </apply>
  </target>


  <target name="phploc" description="Measure project size using
    PHPLOC">
    <exec executable="phploc">
    <arg value="--log-csv" />
    <arg value="${builddir}/logs/phploc.csv" />
    <arg path="${sourcedir}" />
    </exec>
  </target>


  <target name="pdepend" description="Calculate software metrics
    using PHP_Depend">
    <exec executable="pdepend">
      <arg value="--jdepend-xml=${builddir}/logs/jdepend.xml" />
      <arg value="--jdepend-chart=${builddir}/pdepend/dependencies.
svg" />
      <arg value="--overview-pyramid=${builddir}/pdepend/overview-
        pyramid.svg" />
      <arg path="${sourcedir}" />
    </exec>
  </target>


  <target name="phpmd" description="Perform project mess detection
    using PHPMD and print human readable output. Intended for
    usage on the command line before committing.">
    <exec executable="phpmd">
      <arg path="${basedir}/src" />
      <arg value="text" />
      <arg value="${workspace}/app/phpmd.xml" />
    </exec>
  </target>


  <target name="phpmd-ci" description="Perform project mess
    detection using PHPMD creating a log file for the continuous
    integration server">
    <exec executable="phpmd">
      <arg path="${sourcedir}" />
      <arg value="xml" />
```

```
        <arg value="${workspace}/app/phpmd.xml" />
        <arg value="--reportfile" />
        <arg value="${builddir}/logs/pmd.xml" />
    </exec>
</target>

<target name="phpcs" description="Find coding standard
  violations using PHP_CodeSniffer and print human readable
  output. Intended for usage on the command line before
  committing.">
    <exec executable="phpcs">
        <arg value="--standard=Symfony2" />
        <arg path="${sourcedir}" />
    </exec>
</target>

<target name="phpcs-ci" description="Find coding standard
  violations using PHP_CodeSniffer creating a log file for the
  continuous integration server">
    <exec executable="phpcs" output="/dev/null">
        <arg value="--report=checkstyle" />
        <arg value="--report-file=${builddir}/logs/checkstyle.xml" />
        <arg value="--standard=Symfony2" />
        <arg path="${sourcedir}" />
    </exec>
</target>

<target name="phpcpd" description="Find duplicate code using
  PHPCPD">
    <exec executable="phpcpd">
        <arg value="--log-pmd" />
        <arg value="${builddir}/logs/pmd-cpd.xml" />
        <arg path="${sourcedir}" />
    </exec>
</target>

<target name="phpdoc" description="Generate API documentation
  using phpDox">
    <exec executable="phpdoc">
        <arg line="-d '${sourcedir}' -t '${builddir}/docs' --
          title='Tempo' " />
    </exec>
</target>

<target name="phpunit" description="Run unit tests with
```

```
        PHPUnit">
      <exec executable="phpunit" failonerror="true">
        <arg value="-c" />
        <arg path="${basedir}/app/phpunit.xml" />
      </exec>
    </target>

    <target name="phpcb" description="Aggregate tool output with
      PHP_CodeBrowser">
      <exec executable="phpcb">
        <arg value="--log" />
        <arg path="${builddir}/logs" />
        <arg value="--source" />
        <arg path="${sourcedir}" />
        <arg value="--output" />
        <arg path="${builddir}/code-browser" />
      </exec>
    </target>

    <target name="vendors" description="Update vendors">
      <exec executable="composer" failonerror="true">
        <arg value="update" />
      </exec>
    </target>

    <target name="parameters" description="Copy parameters">
      <exec executable="cp" failonerror="true">
        <arg path="app/config/parameters.yml.dist" />
        <arg path="app/config/parameters.yml" />
      </exec>
    </target>

</project>
```

Now create a `build/` subdirectory in the `app/` directory of your project. This is where you keep a configuration file for each PHP tool separately.

Don't go to the `build/` directory yet. While you are still in the `app/` directory, create a `phpmd.xml` file and add the following content to it:

```
<?xml version="1.0"?>
<ruleset name="Symfony2 ruleset"
  xmlns="http://pmd.sf.net/ruleset/1.0.0"
  xmlns:xsi="http://www.w3.org/2001/XMLSchema-instance"
  xsi:schemaLocation="http://pmd.sf.net/ruleset/1.0.0 "
  xsi:noNamespaceSchemaLocation=
  "http://pmd.sf.net/ruleset_xml_schema.xsd">
  <description>
```

```
      Custom ruleset.
   </description>

   <rule ref="rulesets/design.xml" />
   <rule ref="rulesets/unusedcode.xml" />
   <rule ref="rulesets/codesize.xml" />
   <rule ref="rulesets/naming.xml" />


</ruleset>
```

In the root of your project, rename `phpunit.xml.dist` to `phpunit.xml` and replace the content as follows:

```
<?xml version="1.0" encoding="UTF-8"?>


<!-- http://phpunit.de/manual/4.1/en/appendixes.configuration.html
   -->
<phpunit xmlns:xsi="http://www.w3.org/2001/XMLSchema-instance"
   xsi:noNamespaceSchemaLocation="http://schema.phpunit.de/
      4.1/phpunit.xsd"
            backupGlobals             = "false"
            backupStaticAttributes    = "false"
            colors                    = "true"
            convertErrorsToExceptions = "true"
            convertNoticesToExceptions = "true"
            convertWarningsToExceptions = "true"
            processIsolation          = "false"
            stopOnFailure             = "false"
            syntaxCheck               = "false"
            bootstrap="app/autoload.php"
>
   <php>
     <ini name="error_reporting" value="-1" />
   </php>
   <testsuites>
     <testsuite name="Project Test Suite">
       <directory>tests</directory>
     </testsuite>
   </testsuites>

   <php>
     <server name="KERNEL_DIR" value="app/" />
   </php>
   <logging>
```

```
    <log type="coverage-html" target="build/coverage" title="mava"
      charset="UTF-8" yui="true" highlight="true"
      lowUpperBound="35" highLowerBound="70"/>
    <log type="coverage-clover" target="build/logs/clover.xml"/>
    <log type="junit" target="build/logs/junit.xml"
      logIncompleteSkipped="false"/>
  </logging>
  <filter>
    <whitelist>
      <directory>src</directory>
      <exclude>
        <directory>src/*Bundle/Resources</directory>
        <directory>src/*/*Bundle/Resources</directory>
        <directory>src/*/Bundle/*Bundle/Resources</directory>
      </exclude>
    </whitelist>
  </filter>
</phpunit>
```

Creating a new job in Jenkins

At this stage, the setup and configuration part is over and we are ready to create our first CI job:

1. Log in to your Jenkins application and click on **New Item** in the left navigation bar. Then, choose a name for the job, select **Build a free-style software project**, and press **OK**:

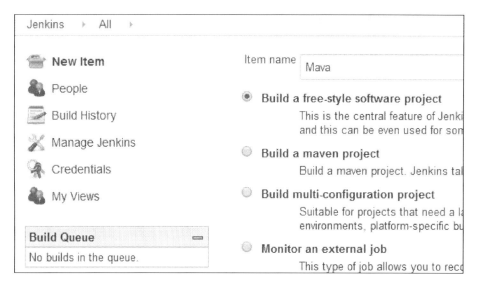

2. Under the **Source Code Management** section, choose **Git** and add
   the `mava` project repository here (The `mava` project is located at
   `git@github.com:Soolan/mava.git`; you are welcome to fork this
   project to your local repository or create a new repository and push
   your own Symfony project here.):

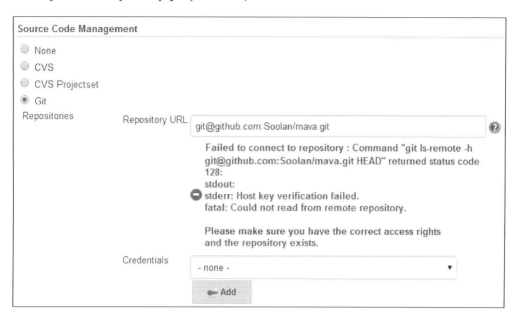

3. As you can see, because of the lack of credentials, an error message is shown.
   To fix the problem, we need to add the Jenkins credentials to our mava
   GitHub repository. In the EC2 instance terminal, log in as Jenkins:

   ```
   $ sudo su - jenkins
   ```

4. Now, generate public/private key pairs:

   ```
   $ ssh-keygen -t dsa
   ```

   ```
   Generating public/private dsa key pair.
   Enter file in which to save the key (/var/lib/jenkins/.ssh/id_
   dsa):
   Enter passphrase (empty for no passphrase):
   Enter same passphrase again:
   Your identification has been saved in /var/lib/jenkins/.ssh/id_
   dsa.
   Your public key has been saved in /var/lib/jenkins/.ssh/id_dsa.
   pub.
   The key fingerprint is:
   ```

```
3d:23:cd:97:8f:60:60:27:5d:a8:c9:fc:de:fb:34:e1 jenkins@ip-172-31-
29-153
The key's randomart image is:
+--[ DSA 1024]----+
|             ..   |
|             ...  |
|         o+oo     |
|         .=B   .  |
|         S.O o .  |
|          o.= + . |
|           . .. E |
|            . ... |
|              .o. |
+-----------------+
```

5. Now copy the public key content to the clipboard:

    ```
    $ cat ~/.ssh/id_dsa.pub | xclip
    ```

6. Go to your GitHub repository, choose the **Settings** tab, and select **Deploy keys** from the left navigation bar. Click on the **Add deploy key** button. Then, in the text area that appears, paste the content of id_dsa.pub:

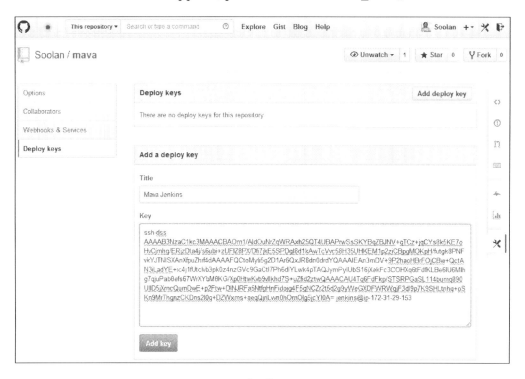

7. When you press the **Add key** button, you are first asked for your GitHub repository password and then you can see the deployed key on the list:

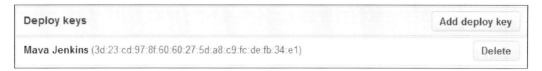

8. Now, go back to Jenkins and copy the failing command on error message:

9. Go to the terminal (with Jenkins as user) and run the copied command:

```
jenkins@ip-172-31-29-153:~$ git ls-remote -h git@github.
com:Soolan/mava.git HEAD
```

```
The authenticity of host 'github.com (192.30.252.130)' can't be
established.
```

```
RSA key fingerprint is 16:27:ac:a5:76:28:2d:36:63:1b:56:4d:eb:df
:a6:48.
```

```
Are you sure you want to continue connecting (yes/no)? yes
```

```
Warning: Permanently added 'github.com,192.30.252.130' (RSA) to
the list of known hosts.
```

10. Head back to Jenkins and remove the GitHub repository. If you enter the repository this time, you can see that the error message will be gone. That's how Jenkins talks to GitHub.

11. Scroll down to **Build Triggers** and check the option as shown in the following image:

12. Under the **Build** section, click on **Add build step** drop down list and select **Invoke Ant**. This will use Ant as the task manager. Clearly, we need to install Ant before we are able to use it in Jenkins. So, on the instance terminal, run the following command:

```
$ sudo apt-get install ant
```

13. Scroll down to the **Post-build Actions** section and select **E-mail Notification** from the list. As you may have noticed, the e-mail notification won't show up until you save the current settings first and open the settings again. Now, you can enter e-mail(s) of recipient(s). If there is more than one recipient, separate the e-mails with a comma. Select all the checkboxes in this section and, at the end, press the **Save** button:

Running the first build

This is the moment of truth. In the past 30 pages, we installed and configured many packages and libraries to see this moment. To see how Jenkins works, click on the **Build Now** button and watch the build process in action:

You can always click on the build link at any time and watch the process live by choosing **Console Output**:

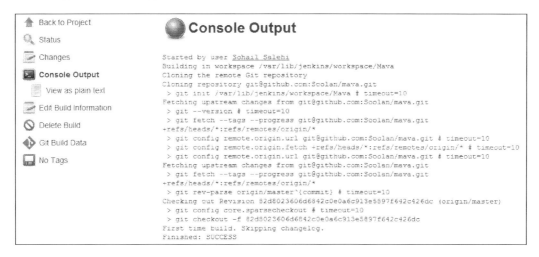

As you can see, the project build has no errors and if you go back to the Jenkins dashboard, you will see the blue success icon that indicates our first build has completed successfully:

It is likely to face a couple of errors before working successfully. As you can see, we have a long list of different things to set up. So a misspelled name or wrong path is not unusual. What I encourage you to do is read the error message carefully, go to the line number in the `build.xml` file, and see how you can fix it.

Sometimes, you may need to work around it. You might copy executable files to your `/usr/local/bin` folder and change the XML file accordingly. I tried to use AWS as a platform for all of us to minimize possible errors and situations. However, it does not guarantee a challenge-free configuration process. To be honest, it took me 14 attempts to finally get Jenkins going. So don't be discouraged if it didn't work at the first attempt.

How does GitHub alert Jenkins about new pushes?

If you remember from the *Configuring Jenkins* section of this chapter, we defined a build trigger as follows:

Build when a change is pushed to GitHub. In other words, Jenkins starts doing its job as soon as it finds out there are some new changes in the code.

There is one problem here. Can you spot it? Yes, that's correct; it sounds like one-way communication. GitHub allows Jenkins to pull new changes, but how on earth should Jenkins know *when* to pull the new changes?

1. To fix this issue, go to the **Settings** tab in your GitHub repository, click on **Webhooks & Services** from the left navigation menu, and choose **Jenkins (Git plugin)** under the **Services** section.

2. Now enter your Jenkins server URL on the next page:

3. Now, go back to Jenkins settings and check **Poll SCM** under **Build Triggers** with the following value and save:

These settings tell Jenkins to poll GitHub frequently and, in case there are new pushes, to pull them to the Jenkins server and get on with the build process. Now they are talking.

To test this, open one of your Symfony templates and make some changes. For example, let's add a line to the bottom of the about template:

```
// src/mava/CoreBundle/Resources/views/About/index.html.twig
{% if name %}
  {{name}} is a member of our team.
{% else %}
  mava is a web app for task management and team collaboration. <br/>
{% endif %}

{{ 'Jenkins Rocks!!!' }}
```

Now save, commit, and push the changes to the GitHub repository:

```
$ git commit -a -m "checking communications"
$ git push
```

Look at your Jenkins. As soon as the push command comes through, Jenkins automatically schedules a new build and executes the required tasks:

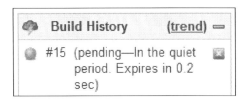

Do I need CI?

A wise man once said, if you want to have a caring, productive, and supportive team in your IT company, ask people to do different tasks at least once a month. Ask the system administrator to sit by a customer support member for a day. Ask developers to sit on a system administrator's chair and ask a customer support member to manage the company for a day.

It might sound scary, but surprisingly, people start seeing daily problems from a totally different perspective and sometimes offer creative solutions that cannot be offered by a professional just because he/she is blinded by so many years of solving problems in the usual way.

This was the purpose of this chapter. Look at the title of this book one more time. You can not master Symfony if, as a developer, you are not willing to explore behind the scenes of CI for a Symfony project. You need to know about the latest technology and tools offered by big boys like Amazon and you need to learn how to utilize them in your projects. It might take a while to digest all of the information provided here. Take your time and spend a week or two reviewing CI concepts. When you fully understand the foundation, you will see how easy and sweet project development will be and how productive you will become.

We are not completely done with CI settings. Remember those PHP libraries that we installed at some stage? As we go through actual PHP development during the chapters to come, I will show you how to use these libraries to spot problems efficiently, generate reports, and define automated tasks based on your project needs.

Summary

In this chapter, you learned about the necessity of the CI server and how it can be beneficial to any project. We saw how to use cloud services such as AWS to host a CI server. We went through the nitty-gritty of CI configurations and the way in which it talks to our code repositories.

The next chapter is about another development methodology that is called Behavior-driven Development and tools and bundles that integrate this feature into a Symfony project.

4
Using Behavior-Driven Development in Symfony

To have a successful and satisfying career as a developer, communication is vital. You might experience a situation where the result of your development efforts was not good enough to make your client happy. Reasons such as misunderstanding a request, constantly changing the development ground, lack of effective testing procedures, and so on cause a project to fail. If you look closer, you will see that communication is the key and can solve many problems before they even happen.

You might be a good developer and communicate with and understand your fellow developers very well. There might be an amazing project manager who communicates with the client clearly. However, how clear is it when it comes to communication between technical and non-technical members of a project?

In this chapter, we will cover the following topics:

- A common language called Gherkin, which is very easy to understand and helps technical and non-technical people talk to each other clearly

- How to use Gherkin in Behat, which is a PHP package for Behavior-Driven Development, in order to define crystal-clear project features and write clever scenarios that are agreeable and acceptable for both parties

- How to use Mink, which is another PHP package to handle browser-related activities and test scenarios created for each feature

Getting started with BDD

Behavior-Driven Development (BDD) is a software development process introduced by Dan North to clarify the purpose of a development request and simplify acceptance tests. In BDD, you basically define a feature for a project in plain and human readable sentences and, when it is accepted by everyone, then you start creating the required code to implement that feature.

In contrast to this, in **Test-Driven Development** (TDD), it is not unusual to be carried away by many unnecessary tests. As you know, in TDD, you have to write a failing test first and then develop the code to pass the test. The question is how would you know that you are heading in the right direction? In other words, how can you be sure that the test you have created in the first place is beneficial to your project? Yes, of course, you can do things right by creating those tests first. However, doing things right is totally different from doing right things. Again, it is all about the money and your client would not be happy to waste their resources on unnecessary things.

BDD was invented to improve the testing experience. You can visualize it as one step above TDD. You define a feature in plain and simple English (or any other human language), make an agreement on it, and then get involved in the implementation and testing details. It is like a compass that helps you find the right direction before fighting wind and waves.

Is BDD a replacement for TDD?

Absolutely not! There might still be some debates about the relationship between BDD and TDD. Keep in mind that BDD is not a replacement for TDD. They work together to improve the idea of acceptance tests. You still need to test your methods and classes (unit testing), but before that, you need to make sure that your application functions the way it is defined and agreed (functional testing).

Long story short, for functional testing, we will use **Behat**, **Mink**, and a few browser emulators and this is where we engage in BDD.

For unit testing, we will use **PHPUnit** and a group of related packages that we have set up on our CI server already (*Chapter 3*, *Setting Up the Environment*) and this is where TDD happens.

Later in this chapter, we will introduce **Codeception** and move all sorts of tests in one integrated and easy-to-use environment.

What is Behat?

Behat is a BDD framework for PHP projects. When you run it for the first time, it reads a text file containing a project feature description written in a human readable language, and because there is no code written yet, it fails the tests and generates the required steps to achieve the goal for that feature.

These generated steps are actually empty PHP methods. Your job is to write the code for each step. (We will deal with that shortly.) Assuming that the code is in place, by running Behat for the second time, it will go through all the required steps one more time and check whether that feature passes all tests. To see Behat in action, let's start by installing it.

Installing and configuring Behat

To get the basic Behat software (and its related libraries) up and running is a simple two-step process. Just add them to your `composer.json` file:

```
"require-dev": {
  // ...
  "behat/behat": "dev-master",
  "behat/mink-extension": "dev-master",
  "behat/mink": "dev-master",
  "behat/mink-selenium2-driver": "dev-master",
  "behat/symfony2-extension": "dev-master",
  "behat/mink-browserkit-driver": "dev-master",
  "behat/mink-goutte-driver": "dev-master"
},
```

Run the following command:

```
$ composer update
```

After downloading the required package, this command creates an executable file in the `bin` directory.

Before initializing Behat, we need to configure it by telling it which plugins we are interested in and where the base URL of our project is. Create a `behat.yml` file in the root of your project and add these lines to it:

```
# /var/www/mava/behat.yml
default:
  extensions:
    Behat\Symfony2Extension: ~
    Behat\MinkExtension:
```

```
goutte: ~
selenium2: ~
base_url: http://localhost:8000/app_dev.php
```

We will look at each line beneath the extensions in the Mink topic. For now, just initialize Behat for your Symfony bundle as follows:

$ bin/behat

By checking your project directory structure, you will notice that there is a new folder in the root called `features`. This is where you create those plain text files that define the project's features. For example, if you want to check the login functionality, you have to create a `features/login.feature` file.

There is a subdirectory called `features/bootstrap`. The real tests happen in this subdirectory. We will see how to define a feature and its required steps soon. For now, let's think about all the possible features for the `mava` project.

The features we need for this project

This is a task management application. So, while I think about features that my application should have, a few keywords such as project, task, member, and workspace pop into my mind. Now, based on these keywords, I can create a mind map and organize my thoughts:

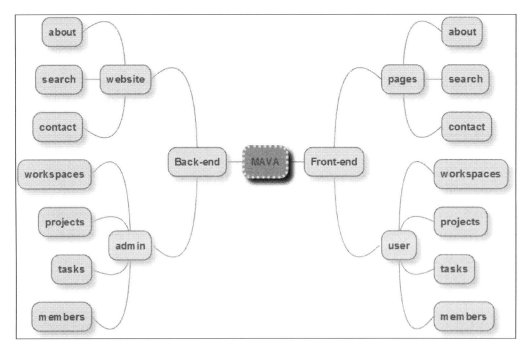

Keep in mind that ideally your client has thought about what he wants and made a few sketches for each page element and functionality. For the purpose of this book, let's pretend that I'm your client and I'm asking you to build a **Minimum Viable Product** (**MVP**) around my idea. To make it challenging, I will act like a non-technical, bossy, and greedy client. All I will provide is that general mind map and, basically, I don't have anything to represent the structure of each page. I have the details in my mind, but it is up to your art of communication to extract this critical information and turn that idea into a web application.

Looking at the mind map, you can see two groups of features. It seems the frontend features include showing some pages to non-authenticated users and providing access to authenticated users for specific pages. The backend does the same except it is for website administrators only. Let's see how to clarify these features by communicating to the client (me).

More information about the project

Let's say we had a meeting and I explained what I'm looking for and you summarized the project facts as follows:

- This is an MVP, so we need to make the project work with some minimum and basic functionality

- It is a web application for task management and contains workspace, project, task, and member entities

- Each task belongs to one project only but each project may contain multiple tasks

- Each project can be defined in one workspace only but each workspace can have multiple projects

- Each task can be assigned to one member only but each member can have multiple tasks

- The frontend pages include a contact us page, static about page, search box, which is redirected to a search result page, and login/register form, which will be redirected to user account/user registration pages

- The backend is the same but only users with administrative roles can access it

- Task entity contains these properties: title, description, due date, and attachments

- Project entity contains these properties: title, description, and due date

- Member entity contains these properties: name, role, e-mail, and password

- Workspace entity contains these properties: title and description
- User should be able to log in to their account and manage their own workspaces, projects, tasks, and members
- Administrator should be able to log in to the backend and manage website static pages plus everyone's workspaces, projects, tasks, and members

So, we had the meeting and you bullet-pointed your understanding of the project. Now let's convert these features to a common language and see if we are on the same page.

Gherkin – the common language

The Behat framework was originally inspired by the Cucumber project, which is the BDD framework for Ruby. So don't be surprised that the language to explain project features is called **Gherkin**. Gherkin is a simple language created to describe features in a human readable format.

Here is a sample code written in Gherkin:

```
Feature: about page
    In order to see about page contents
    As a user
    I am able to visit about page
```

It does look ridiculously obvious, doesn't it? Isn't clarity what we wanted? Don't let its simplicity trick you. As we proceed, you will see that there is a lot of power behind it. Here is what's happening in the previous code snippet:

- The first line is the feature title. Choose something relevant to your feature.
- The second line explains the benefit or value of that feature—what it does for our project. It will become very handy by the time you finish writing all the features and want to prioritize them.
- The third line indicates the person/concept that will benefit from it.
- The last line explains briefly how it is going to happen.

The about page feature on its own doesn't do anything. In order to see this feature in action, we need to add some scenarios to it.

Writing a scenario for the about page

A scenario is basically a possible situation where features can act upon. This means that each feature can have many scenarios. Consider the about page that we created in *Chapter 2*, *The Request and Response Life Cycle*. When you visit /about, you see a general about page. When you visit /about/{name}, there are two possible scenarios: if {name} exists, you see their about page and if it doesn't, you see an error page. So we have three possible scenarios for the /about page. Let's add them to our feature and see how it looks:

```
Feature: about page
   In order to see about page contents
   As a user
   I am able to visit about page

   Scenario: Visiting about page
   Given I am on "/about"
   Then I should see "mava is a web app"

   Scenario: Visiting about page for an existing user
   Given I am on "/about/john"
   Then I should see "He is a cool guy"

   Scenario: Visiting about page for non existing user
   Given I am on "/about/jim"
   Then I should see "Not Found"
```

As you can see, each scenario starts with the keyword Scenario: followed by the title for it. Each line after that represents a step for that scenario. Here, we have seen the simplest form of it as a two-step scenario. The Given keyword demonstrates the scene (the requirement) for our scenario. The Then keyword explains the outcome of the scenario.

There are other keywords (When, And, and But) in Gherkin and I will show you how to use them as we proceed.

Seeing it in action

Now that we have a feature with three possible scenarios, let's see how it works:

1. Choose a name for this feature and save the feature in the following directory:

    mava/features/about.feature

2. Open `/features/bootstrap/FeatureContext.php` and modify the class as follows:

```php
<?php
//...
use Behat\MinkExtension\Context\MinkContext;

class FeatureContext extends MinkContext
{
    //...
}
```

I will talk about Mink and what it does soon.

3. Run the feature:

```
$ bin/behat
```

After running Behat, it looks in the `features` folder and opens the `about.feature` file. Then, it will go through every step defined in each `Scenario`, ask Mink to evaluate the contents of each page, and see if it matches with the value provided.

Behind the scenes, Mink will use a browser emulator called **Goutte** to check the URL provided in each scenario and read the response contents for each page.

In this feature, we have three scenarios and six steps, and as you can see, all of them passed successfully. Here is the output of that command:

```
Feature: about page
  In order to see about page contents
  As a user
  I am able to visit about page

  Scenario: Visiting about page                      # features/about.feature:7
    Given I am on "/about"                            # FeatureContext::visit()
    Then I should see "mava is a web app"             # FeatureContext::assertPageContainsText()

  Scenario: Visiting about page for an existing user  # features/about.feature:12
    Given I am on "/about/john"                       # FeatureContext::visit()
    Then I should see "He is a cool guy"              # FeatureContext::assertPageContainsText()

  Scenario: Visiting about page for non existing user # features/about.feature:17
    Given I am on "/about/jim"                         # FeatureContext::visit()
    Then I should see "Not Found"                     # FeatureContext::assertPageContainsText()

3 scenarios (3 passed)
6 steps (6 passed)
0m0.36s (16.92Mb)
```

Headless versus zombie

With our first feature test passed, now is the perfect time to study the `behat.yml` file:

```
# /var/www/mava/behat.yml
default:
  extensions:
    Behat\Symfony2Extension: ~
    Behat\MinkExtension:
      goutte: ~
      selenium2: ~
      base_url: http://mava.dev/app_dev.php
```

Under the `extensions` key, there are two entries: `Symfony2Extention` is used to integrate Behat into Symfony projects and `MinkExtension` is where the real acceptance tests happen. Technically, Mink is a framework that forces a browser emulator or browser controller to do what it says.

A headless browser emulator such as Goutte does not have any GUI attached. That's why it is called headless. It runs from the command line and, because it has no window, it is very light and fast. As you saw in the previous topic, checking all three scenarios took a fraction of a second (look at the last line of the previous image). The drawback is that you cannot test JavaScript calls in it.

On the other hand, a browser controller forces a real browser to open a window, fill in the forms, click on buttons, and do anything you normally do while surfing the web. As it can force (zombify) the browser to do these tasks automatically, it is called a browser controller. **Selenium2** is one of the best browser controllers in the world, and **Zombie.js** is another popular one. The good news is that they are capable of handling JavaScript libraries.

As we don't want to deal with every headless or zombie directly, we ask Mink to harness their power and use it to our benefit. As you can see in the `behat.yml` file, we have `goutte` and `selenium2` entries defined under the `MinkExtension` key. We saw how Goutte works; let's see how to use Selenium2.

Using the Selenium2 controller for automated tests

We need to install Selenium2 first and to do so follow the steps:

1. Download the Selenium2 driver:

   http://www.seleniumhq.org/download/

2. Run it by executing the following:

```
$ java -jar ~/Downloads/selenium-server-standalone-[latest-
version].jar
```

3. Now edit the `features/about.feature` file as follows:

```
Feature: about page
  In order to see about page contents
  As a user
  I am able to visit about page

  @javascript
  Scenario: Visiting about page
  Given I am on "/about"
  Then I should see "mava is a web app"

  @javascript
  Scenario: Visiting about page for an existing user
  Given I am on "/about/john"
  Then I should see "He is a cool guy"

  @javascript
  Scenario: Visiting about page for non existing user
  Given I am on "/about/jim"
  Then I should see "Not Found"
```

Adding an `@javascript` annotation before each scenario means that we need a browser controller. So Mink will look into its drivers and choose Selenium2 over Goutte.

4. Now run the tests again:

```
$ bin/behat
```

You will see that for each scenario, a browser window opens automatically and a page related to the specified URL is loaded.

> By default, Selenium2 uses Firefox. So you need to have it installed in your machine. It is possible to use any other browser if you wish. To do so, install your desired browser driver and set up a config file to choose that driver. See the Selenium documentation for more details:
>
> `http://www.seleniumhq.org/docs/`

The about page does not follow BDD

The process so far is politically correct but technically it does not satisfy what I promised at the beginning of this chapter. In BDD, we are supposed to define a feature and its scenarios first, and then start coding. Well, the about page and its variations have been developed in *Chapter 2*, *The Request and Response Life Cycle*, already. The reason I chose them was only to show BDD elements in action. However, don't worry, we will start afresh and completely get rid of the about page and whatever attached to it soon.

In other words, in the chapters to come, we won't jump into coding for anything unless it has been defined and prioritized as a feature and some crystal-clear scenarios have been written for it. This chapter is just an introduction to BDD and we cannot cover everything here. So for now, we will leave some topics such as how to create scenario outlines, parametric scenarios, backgrounds, and so on for later and come back to them in a practical situation later.

Knowing how BDD generally works, let's create a scenario for something that does not exist yet. This way, we will see how Behat and Mink interact with each other.

As your client, imagine that I ask you to hide part of the about page for each member and show it only by pressing a button. Currently, we have a name, biography, and e-mail for each member. However, in the future, there might be a lot of fields. So being able to show them on demand will probably make the page look more tidy and organized.

A scenario to show the user's details

Get rid of all the scenarios in `about.feature` except the second one and modify it as follows:

```
Feature: about page
   In order to see about page contents
   As a user
   I am able to visit about page

   @javascript
   Scenario: showing details of an existing user in about page
   Given I am on "/about/john"
   When I press more
   Then I should see "email"
```

There is a new step here called `When`. This step contains the action that the user will take in the scenario and the action here is pressing a button.

Now open `feautures/bootstrap/FeatureContext.php` and make it implement the snippet class while it is still extending `MinkContext`:

```php
<?php
// ...
use Behat\MinkExtension\Context\MinkContext;
class FeatureContext extends MinkContext implements
    SnippetAcceptingContext
{
    /...
}
```

If you run Behat now, you will see a different response:

```
Feature: about page
  In order to see about page contents
  As a user
  I am able to visit about page

  Scenario: showing details of an existing user in about page  # features/about.feature:12
    Given I am on "/about/john"                                # FeatureContext::visit()
    When I press the details button
    Then I should see "email"                                  # FeatureContext::assertPageContainsText()

1 scenario (1 undefined)
3 steps (1 passed, 1 undefined, 1 skipped)
0m0.12s (16.71Mb)

--- FeatureContext has missing steps. Define them with these snippets:

    /**
     * @When I press the details button
     */
    public function iPressTheDetailsButton()
    {
        throw new PendingException();
    }
```

Let's talk about the details of each step:

- The **Given** step (green line) passed successfully because we have implemented the /about/john page in *Chapter 2, The Request and Response Life Cycle*, already

- The **When** step (orange line) is undefined, which means that we don't have the details button yet, and it is our job to create it

- The **Then** step (blue line) was skipped because it depends on the `When` step

At the end of this output, there is a code snippet for the missing step. If you look at the `FeatureContext` class, you will see that it implements `SnippetAcceptingContext`. Thanks to this interface, we had that snippet generated for us. All you need to do is copy this method and paste it in the `FeatureContext` class or, instead of doing it manually, you can ask Behat to do it for you:

```
$ bin/behat --append-snippets
```

Now check your `FeatureContext` class and you will see a new method over there:

```php
<?php
// ...
class FeatureContext extends MinkContext implements
  SnippetAcceptingContext
{
  /...
  /**
   * @When I press more
   */
  public function iPressMore()
  {
    throw new PendingException();
  }
}
```

This will be our blueprint for development. By running Behat again, you will see that the **undefined** step has turned to **pending** now:

```
Feature: about page
  In order to see about page contents
  As a user
  I am able to visit about page

  Scenario: showing details of an existing user in about page  # features/about.feature:12
    Given I am on "/about/john"                                 # FeatureContext::visit()
    When I press the details button                             # FeatureContext::iPressTheDetailsButton()
      TODO: write pending definition
    Then I should see "email"                                   # FeatureContext::assertPageContainsText()

1 scenario (1 pending)
3 steps (1 passed, 1 pending, 1 skipped)
0m0.12s (16.71Mb)
```

Let's summarize what just happened. We defined a feature in a human readable language and created a scenario for it. The client can understand it and the developer can understand it and, based on this language, Behat generated a code snippet (a blueprint, if you like) for the developer. Now that we have a clear direction to go in, the development process feels easy and straightforward and, more importantly, feels closer to the BDD idea.

Implementing the user's details scenario

Let's start by modifying the user template:

1. Open the `user.html.twig` file and change it as follows:

```
{# mava/src/AppBundle/Resouces/views/About/user.html.twig #}
<h1>User Profile</h1>
<strong>Name: </strong>{{user.name}} <br/>
<strong>Bio: </strong>{{user.bio}} <br/>
<button
  type="button"
  onclick="location.href='{{ path('about', {'name':
  user.name}) }}'">
  more
  </button>
```

2. In the same place, create a new template and add the following content to it:

```
{# mava/src/AppBundle/Resouces/views/About/more.html.twig #}
<h1>User Profile</h1>
<strong>Name: </strong>{{user.name}} <br/>
<strong>email: </strong>{{user.email}} <br/>
<strong>Bio: </strong>{{user.bio}} <br/>
```

3. Now define a new route for it:

```
{# mava/src/AppBundle/Resouces/config/routing.yml #}
app_about_more:
  path:     /about/{name}/details
  defaults: { _controller: AppBundle:About:details}
```

4. Finally create a new action in the `AboutController` class for it:

```
// mava/src/AppBundle/Controller/AboutController.php
class AboutController extends Controller{
  public function detailsAction($name)
  {
  $user=$this->getDoctrine()
        ->getRepository('AppBundle:User')
        ->findOneByName($name);
  return $this->render(
        'AppBundle:About:more.html.twig',
        array('user' => $user)
        );
  }
```

It is not the best way to implement it but for our testing purposes, it is quick and easy. By visiting the `http://localhost:8000/about/john` URL, you will see that the e-mail field has disappeared and there is a **more** button instead and pressing the button reveals the e-mail. Now let's see how Mink does the acceptance tests.

Testing the scenario

We just implemented the `When` step of our scenario, which means that we need to change the pending mode to something functional. Open the `FeatureContext.php` file and edit it as follows:

```
// mava/features/bootstrap/FeatureContext.php
<?php
//...
class FeatureContext extends MinkContext implements
  SnippetAcceptingContext
{
  //...
  /**
   * @When I press the details button
   */
  public function iPressTheDetailsButton()
  {
    //throw new PendingException();
    $this->getSession()          // the browser
      ->getPage()                // the DocumentElement
      ->findButton("more")       // the NodeElement
      ->press();                 // what you want to do with it
  }
}
```

The class extended from Mink so that we have access to a lot of methods, which I will go through as we proceed. In the example, we have `getSession()`. Whenever you see the word session in your BDD tests, it means browser (a driver instance). As we used the `@javascript` annotation in our scenario, Mink is going to use Selenium2 to force Firefox to do something for us.

The `getPage()` returns the current page. Consider any `Page()` object as a DOM. It contains all the HTML elements of the current page. As our scenario says that we are on the `/about/john` page (the `Given` step), we can traverse the nodes and do whatever we like.

The `findButton("more")` acts like a jQuery selector and finds an element for us. There are a few other methods in the `find()` family, which I will show later. Here, we explicitly aimed for a button. Now we found the button and by calling the `press()` method, simulated the button push action, which led us to the `/about/john/details` page.

If you run Behat again, you will see that a browser window opens automatically, the `/about/john` page is visited, the **more** button is pushed, and the `details` page is shown. At the end, the browser window will close automatically. Looking at the acceptance test results, we can see that all three steps passed successfully:

```
Feature: about page
  In order to see about page contents
  As a user
  I am able to visit about page

  @javascript
  Scenario: showing details of an existing user in about page # features/about.feature:12
    Given I am on "/about/john"                               # FeatureContext::visit()
    When I press the details button                           # FeatureContext::iPressTheDetailsButton()
    Then I should see "email"                                 # FeatureContext::assertPageContainsText()

1 scenario (1 passed)
3 steps (3 passed)
0m6.20s (16.27Mb)
```

> There is a shortcut to find and press a button in one call. You can use the following approach if you like:
>
> ```
> $this->getSession()->getPage()->pressButton('more');
> ```

More about the acceptance test flow in Mink

As you saw in the previous topic, an acceptance test with Mink is all about finding elements in a page and checking to see whether they do what is expected from them. Behind the scenes, there are four important Mink objects that carry a lot of heavy lifting for us:

- `Driver`: The `Driver` class implements `Behat\Mink\Driver\DriverInterface`, and Mink deals with every browser emulator or browser controller through this interface. We have two drivers installed in our project (Goutte and Selenium2), but keep in mind that the current version of Mink comes with five drivers out of the box.

- `Session`: Controlling the browser happens through the `Session` object. This is where Mink sends HTTP requests and listens for responses.

- `DocumentElement`: This is the actual web page containing all the page elements.

- `NodeElement`: Through this object, you can access and manipulate all the elements in a page.

In general, the acceptance test workflow looks something like this:

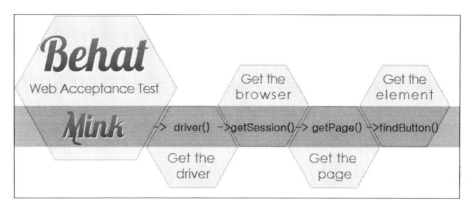

Defining and prioritizing features

Considering the mind map at the beginning of this chapter and knowing some facts about the `mava` project, we can write some feature files in Gherkin. Let's start with the backend:

```
# workspace.feature
Feature: Workspace administration
  In order to manage workspaces
  As an admin
  I am able to see, add, edit and delete workspaces in the backend
```

Some possible scenarios for this feature would be as follows:

```
@javascript
Scenario: seeing a list of available workspaces
Given I am logged in as admin
And There are 3 workspaces
And I am on "/admin"
When I click on "Workspaces"
Then I should see 3 items in the table

@javascript
Scenario: adding a new workspace
```

```
Given I am logged in as admin
And I am on "/admin/workspaces"
When I click on "New"
And I fill the "Title" with "My Workspace"
And I fill the "Description" with "Testing add functionality"
And I press "save"
Then I should see "New workspace created"

@javascript
Scenario: editing a workspace
Given I am logged in as admin
And I am on "/admin/workspaces"
When I click on "edit"
And I fill the "Title" with "edited title"
And I fill the "Description" with "edited description"
And I press "save"
Then I should see "All changes are saved"

@javascript
Scenario: deleting a workspace
Given I am logged in as admin
And I am on "/admin/workspaces"
When I click on "delete"
And I press "yes"
Then I should see "The workspace has been removed"
```

With the examples that you have seen so far, these Gherkin commands make sense now, don't they? The rest of the features are similar. I'm not going to write all of them here. Instead, we will pick a few of them in each chapter, write all the possible scenarios for each, and start development till they pass functional and unit tests. For now, keep in mind that for the purposes of this book, backend features (administrative area first and website next) have a higher priority compared to the frontend.

Codeception – the BDD style testing framework

I would like to introduce another PHP testing framework that has an easier learning curve and some unique features to create unit, functional, and acceptance tests.

In Codeception—unlike Behat—we don't need to write the scenarios in another language (Gherkin) and all the steps of test scenarios will be written in PHP. This is one of the main reasons for debates on the Behat versus Codeception topic. If you search for it on Google, you will find that there is a war going on out there. I have used and will use both of them in my personal projects. I won't compare and recommend one over another. They both have their own strengths and weaknesses, and it is totally up to you to decide which one you are comfortable with.

In this topic, I will talk about installing, bootstrapping, and creating a few tests in Codeception and, in the chapters to come, the main focus will be on Symfony itself. In other words, tests, no matter which framework you are going to choose, will be kept in the `tests/` folder at the root of your project and should have the same effect no matter which test framework you choose.

 Did you know that you can install and use both Behat and Codeception frameworks side by side in your project?

Installing the Codeception framework

Before installation, the first thing that I want you to do is go to the root of your project and delete the `tests/` folder completely. This folder will be created again by Codeception and we will add our own tests as we go. Now install Codeception via Composer as follows:

```
$ composer require "codeception/codeception"
```

This command will install the latest stable version of Codeception and required dependencies in your `vendor` directory.

Bootstrapping Codeception

Now we need to create a directory structure (bootstrap) for our tests. Look at the `vendor/bin` directory and you will find a bunch of binary files, including `codecept` that we will use for command-line calls. For example, to initialize Codeception for our project, we will use the following command:

```
$ vendor/bin/codecept bootstrap
```

The output confirms that a couple of files and folders are created under the `tests/` directory and there is a configuration file called `codeception.yml` at the root of our project:

```
Initializing Codeception in /var/www/packt/mava

File codeception.yml created        <- global configuration

tests/unit created                  <- unit tests

tests/unit.suite.yml written        <- unit tests suite configuration

tests/functional created            <- functional tests

tests/functional.suite.yml written <- functional tests suite
configuration

tests/acceptance created            <- acceptance tests

tests/acceptance.suite.yml written <- acceptance tests suite
configuration

tests/_output was added to .gitignore

  ---

tests/_bootstrap.php written <- global bootstrap file
Building initial Tester classes
Building Actor classes for suites: unit, functional, acceptance
  -> UnitTesterActions.php generated successfully. 0 methods added
\UnitTester includes modules: Asserts, \Helper\Unit
UnitTester.php created.
  -> FunctionalTesterActions.php generated successfully. 0 methods added
\FunctionalTester includes modules: \Helper\Functional
FunctionalTester.php created.
  -> AcceptanceTesterActions.php generated successfully. 0 methods added
\AcceptanceTester includes modules: PhpBrowser, \Helper\Acceptance
AcceptanceTester.php created.
```

If you check out the `/var/www/packt/mava/tests` directory, you will see the newly created files here:

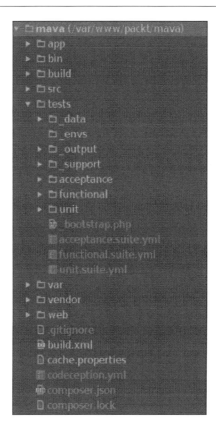

Test suits

Let's skip the configuration files and folders for now, (I will come back to them as we proceed) and focus on the following folders only:

```
tests/acceptance/
```

```
tests/functional/
```

```
tests/unit/
```

These folders hold the code for acceptance, function, and unit tests respectively. Looking at each folder, we will find that they have an empty bootstrap file at the moment. This file will be the home for extra test-related settings that we need in the future.

For now, let's create two simple unit and functional tests for our `DefaultController`. Run the following commands to create these tests:

```
$ vendor/bin/codecept generate:test unit DefaultController
$ vendor/bin/codecept generate:cest functional DefaultController
```

In these commands, we generated the tests and saved them in their related folders (suits). You might have noticed that in the real filename, the type of test is mentioned at the end of the file. For example, `generate:test unit` creates a test file in the `unit/` folder as follows:

```
/tests/unit/DefaultControllerTest.php
```

The `generate:cest functional` command creates a test file in the `functional/` folder as follows:

```
/tests/functional/DefaultControllerCest.php
```

Apart from `generate:test` and `generate:cest` generators, there are two other commands to generate test files.

- `generate:cept`: This will have the same effect as the `cest` command except that the test structure will be created in a plain coding style and you won't see any classes or objects.
- `generate:phpunit`: This will create the pure PHPUnit-style test. Keep in mind that Codeception unit tests (`generate:test`) are extended traditional PHPUnit tests and have added some methods on top of that. We will see them in action in the chapters to come.

So, to recap, the following are the four test file generators:

- `generate:cept`
- `generate:cest`
- `generate:test`
- `generate:phpunit`

 Did you know that you can use g instead of `generate` to keep commands shorter?

```
vendor/bin/codecept g:test unit [testfilename]
```

We will choose `cest` over `cept` because `cest` creates a class style for the tests, and we will choose `test` over `phpunit` because, apart from the usual PHPUnit methods, it has a few extra methods that will make our life a lot easier.

 While generating `cest` files, it is important to keep the last part of the name, `[SomeControlName] Cest`, as it is, because that's how Codeception recognizes these functional test files. If you remove the last part, that test won't be executed.

The testers

Check the contents of the new test file in `test/functional/DefaultControllerCest.php` and notice the object type, `FunctionalTester`:

```php
<?php
class DefaultControllerCest
{
  public function _before(FunctionalTester $I)
  {
  }

  public function _after(FunctionalTester $I)
  {
  }

  // tests
  public function tryToTest(FunctionalTester $I)
  {
  }
}
```

The `FunctionalTester` object is responsible for calling all functional test-related methods during this course. If you are wondering where this name came from, open the `tests/functional.suite.yml` file and look at the `class_name` key:

```yaml
# tests/functional.suite.yml
class_name: FunctionalTester
modules:
  enabled:
    # add framework module here
    - \Helper\Functional
```

You can change the `class_name` value to whatever makes you happier. Just remember to use the same name in the test class as well. As long as we are here, let's add some configurations. Replace the comment below the `enabled` key with the following lines:

```
modules:
  enabled:
    - Symfony2:
        app_path: 'app'
        var_path: 'var'
        environment: 'test'
```

Why `Symfony2`? Why are we not using Symfony3 in the settings? We are using Symfony3 after all, right? That's because, at the time of writing this chapter, the module name is called `Symfony2` and if you try something else, you will get the following error messages:

```
[Codeception\Exception\ConfigurationException]
  Module Symfony3 could not be found and loaded
```

I believe that, eventually, some modifications will be applied to the Codeception module names and we can use the correct name.

Adding sample tests

It is time to create some unit and functional tests for our `DefaultController`. First of all, unlike the usual Symfony tests, you don't have to follow the same `Bundle/ControllerTest` naming convention to create tests in Codeception. You can call your tests whatever you like and as long as there is the `Cest` part at the end of the test class names, you are good. However, in this book, I will follow the same Symfony naming convention for the sake of readability.

Keeping this in mind, add a new method to the unit test file as follows:

```
// tests/unit/DefaultControllerTest.php
<?php
class DefaultControllerTest extends \Codeception\TestCase\Test
{ // . . .
  public function testAboutAction()
  {
    $this->assertTrue(true);
  }
}
```

We don't need to go deep into testing at the moment, so a simple assertion will do the job. For a functional test, add the following code:

```
// tests/functional/DefaultControllerCest.php
<?php
class DefaultControllerCest
{
  //...
  public function indexActionTest(FunctionalTester $I)
  {
    $I->wantTo('too see the welcome message on home page');
    $I->amOnPage('/');
    $I->see('Welcome');
  }
}
```

This is a very simple test showing an introductory message (using the wantTo() method), making a request to the index page (using the amOnPage('/') method), and checking the response contents looking for the word 'Welcome' (using the see() method). Basically, this is the same BDD scenario, which is written in PHP here.

Running the tests

To run the tests, we simply pass the run option to the codecept command:

```
$ vendor/bin/codecept run
```

This command goes through all three test suits looking for test files and executing them one by one. This is the output when all tests pass successfully:

```
Codeception PHP Testing Framework v2.1.5
Powered by PHPUnit 4.8.22 by Sebastian Bergmann and contributors.


Unit Tests (1) ------------------------------------------------------
Test about action (DefaultControllerTest::testAboutAction)          Ok
---------------------------------------------------------------------


Functional Tests (1) ------------------------------------------------
Too see the welcome message on home page (DefaultControllerCest::indexAct
ionTest)                              Ok
---------------------------------------------------------------------
```

```
Acceptance Tests (0) ------------------------
---------------------------------------------


Time: 588 ms, Memory: 27.00Mb
OK (2 tests, 2 assertions)
```

Other ways of running tests is to specify all the tests in a specific suit:

```
$ vendor/bin/codecept run functional
```

You can also run just one specific test in a specific suit:

```
$ vendor/bin/codecept run unit DefaultControllerTest
```

While running tests, we can ask Codeception to generate the scenario that we have created in PHP in plain English:

```
$ vendor/bin/codecept run functional --steps
```

As you can see, the output is slightly different this time and more descriptive:

```
Functional Tests (1) -------------------------------------------------
Too see the welcome message on home page (DefaultControllerCest::indexAct
ionTest)
Scenario:
* I am on page "/"
* I see "Welcome"
 PASSED
```

This was only an introduction to Codeception and you will learn more about it. For example, we will see how to use Selenium2 for acceptance tests in the following chapters.

Summary

In this chapter, you learned how to revolutionize your development habits by harnessing the power of BDD through Behat and Codeception testing frameworks.

We saw how to use a common human readable language called Gherkin to build a bridge between technical and non-technical members of a project.

We wrote features and scenarios in Gherkin and asked Behat to create code snippets based on them.

You learned how to use Mink to control headless browser emulators and zombified browser controllers in order to do web acceptance tests for us.

We saw how to use Codeception to do the same but with PHP scenarios, and we will see more of Codeception mainly on the subject of acceptance tests, in the chapters to come.

The good news is that the hard part is almost over and from now on, we will immerse ourselves into pure and sweet development tasks.

In the next chapter, we will study the business logic. This involves entities and their relationships with each other and, more importantly, the mechanisms that fetch, modify, and store entities in a database.

5
Business Logic

Business logic (also known as the domain logic) is all about the way business wants to handle the data. With this definition, it seems that the Model layer in a **Model-View-Controller** (**MVC**) framework could be one of the places to deal with business logic. Forget about MVC because Symfony is more like Request/Response in nature. So, it is your responsibility to create the Model if you need and it is totally up to you how to organize the business logic in your project.

There is a debate about Symfony being an MVC framework. Some developers believe that because entities in Symfony are a data-persistence layer and not a model layer, this makes Symfony a VC framework and not an MVC framework. Sure, you can create Models yourself, but that is where the debate comes from. You have to *CREATE* them. They *DON'T EXIST* by default. My thoughts on this? Don't let the terminology trick you. Read about the debates and opposing ideas as much as you can, but at the end of the day, ask yourself two fundamental questions:

- Which definition, idea, tool, or whatever helps you create a practical code?
- Which one of them leads to a cost-effective result when it comes to security and maintenance?

Some people prefer to beef up their controllers with business logic; some prefer to use an entity repository. I personally prefer to create a **Service-Oriented Architecture** (**SOA**) and move part (if not all) of the business logic to services and utilities (custom classes). We will talk about services, service containers, and dependency injection in detail in *Chapter 7, The Presentation Layer*. There, I will explain SOA practically.

However, here is the challenge: moving the business logic to a service sometimes can be tricky and, as we know, this project is supposed to be a **Minimum Viable Product (MVP)** at the beginning. So, if you are going to prototype something fast, it is better to keep the business logic in entity repositories and access them through controllers.

However, in this book, I'm going to give you the best of both worlds. First, we create a business logic like a normal human being and put it where it lazily lives by default. Then, a few chapters later, we turn everything into a service and make our business logic look like it is on steroids. This way, the controllers will be kept lean and clean and business logic will be importable/reusable anywhere else in the world. Building a web application on top of independent services is a well-known development best practice. Yes, I know, it is going to be a bumpy road, but you will feel fantastic at the end. Long story short, if you are not willing to SoC your code, then what is the point of mastering Symfony?

> *"In computer science, **separation of concerns (SoC)** is a design principle for separating a computer program into distinct sections, such that each section addresses a separate concern."*
>
> *– Wikipedia*

So here is the plan for this chapter:

- First, we will talk about the required entities for this project
- Then, based on the relations between entities, we will create the `.orm.yml` configuration files and ask Symfony to generate entities and their empty repositories
- Next, we will write some scenarios for business logic and use Codeception to create the blueprints for the failing tests
- At the end, we will implement, test, and push the code to our GitHub repository, where it wakes up Jenkins and asks him to initiate a new build for us

Choosing between creating a Model or entity

The common mistake among some Symfony developers is that they think an entity is a Model or, even worse, it can be modified to look like a Model. I have seen entities that consist of a bunch of traits and services are injected into some of them. The end result is bulky code, which is hard to maintain and very slow to run.

Adding extra features to an entity is a bad practice. Keep entities as a data-persistence layer and, if you need a Model, create one. There, you can inject the services if you have to.

You might notice some third-party bundles such as FOSUserBundle have another folder called Model and keep objects similar to entities here. They also have extra code, usually called managers, to take care of additional needs and injecting other services.

As a general rule, if you are happy with Doctrine, then use entities. However, if you want your bundle be independent of any persistence layer and have extra features and services injected into your code, use Model. Here, we are definitely going to use a relational database only (MySQL) and we are definitely going to follow the MVP approach. So, it is not necessary to create Models for now. In case you are interested in databases such as MongoDB or NoSQL, then the best practice is to create Model for bundles and decouple the persistence layer from it. This takes a little bit of extra work, of course, but it is one of the best practices as well. The following figure shows the difference between two practices used:

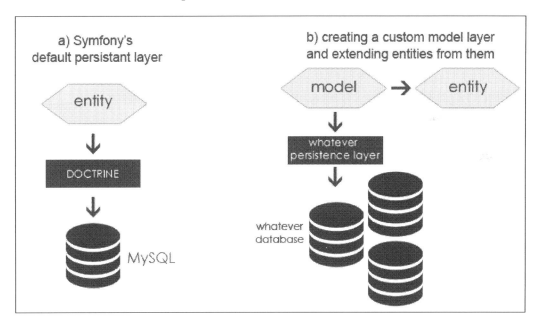

So where does the business logic live?

Let's go back to the definition of business logic again. It defines the business requirements and rules that will be applied to the data. This includes the ways data is created, represented, and modified. To give you a short answer, according to our MVP approach, it lives in our `AppBundle` under the `/Entity` folder. However, later it will move to a couple of services (which can be kept in any folder and can be called globally from anywhere in the project).

Let me clarify the purpose of using **Entity**, **EntityRepository**, and **Service** in our project. Entity represents an object definition for a thing in real life (that is, workspace, project, task, or user). EntityRepository is where you define methods to do database queries (that is, using CRUD on entities). You can do the same in a Service but the difference is that a Service can be called globally anywhere in your project. Moreover, it is instantiated only once and on demand (no matter how many times you call it). This means that it doesn't waste any memory and helps create an optimized project.

Reviewing the facts and building entity relationships

Based on some facts provided in the previous chapter, we have four entities so far: **Workspace**, **Project**, **Task**, and **User**. Each entity (table) has its own properties (columns) and there is some relationship between these entities. For example, each project can be defined in one workspace only but each workspace can have multiple projects or each task can come from one project only but each project can consist of multiple tasks.

This project is all about task management. So, to visualize it better, imagine that workspace is like a playground for all other entities to deal with tasks, as shown in the following figure:

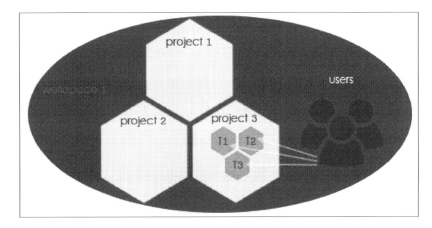

Currently, we are at the MVP level but as we proceed, the entity structure of the project gets bigger and more complex. So, understanding the whole business logic would be much easier if we create a diagram containing all entities, properties, and relationships.

The best way to create a visual concept from the project facts is to use an online or desktop app to create **Entity Relationship Diagrams** (ERDs). You might prefer old-fashioned pen and paper, but in case you want to experiment with gadgets, then places such as `http://erdiagrams.com/` or `https://erdplus.com/#/` might help you. You can use applications such as Lucichart or gliffy too. Just open the **Entity-Relationship** panel in these applications and find all the required tools to create the diagrams you need.

I prefer the Reverse Engineering tool in **MySQL Workbench** because it helps me keep everything organized in one place, and after generating a diagram, I can use it internally to generate tables and vice versa! You can create your tables first and then generate diagrams from them. That's why it is called the Reverse Engineering tool.

There are two strategies to design a software. In the **Bottom-Up** approach, we start with the detailed specifications of small components first and glue them together later to build the whole software. This requires precise information about basic building blocks before starting.

In the **Top-Down** approach, we see the software as a whole concept. We start with a general idea, not knowing the details of each component, and polish it as we go.

The MVP approach in this book, plus the idea of Behavior-Driven Development, strongly suggests that we have to proceed with the Top-Down design.

You can get the latest version of MySQL Workbench at `http://dev.mysql.com/downloads/workbench`.

Creating ERDs using MySQL Workbench

Assuming that you have installed and logged in to your MySQL Workbench, perform the following steps:

1. Choose **Database** | **Reverse Engineer** (*Ctrl + R*) and connect to your local database server.

2. Choose **mava** when it asks for schema:

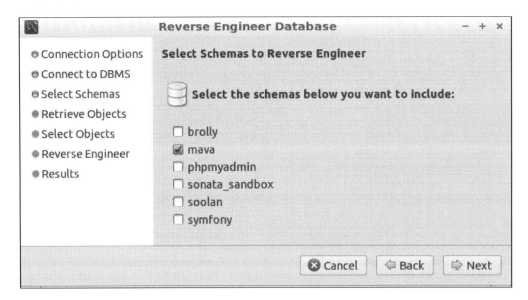

3. Accept all the default settings and click on the **Next** button all the way down to the final step. At the end, you will see that an **EER Diagram** has been generated, **EER** stands for **Enhanced Entity-Relation Diagram**:

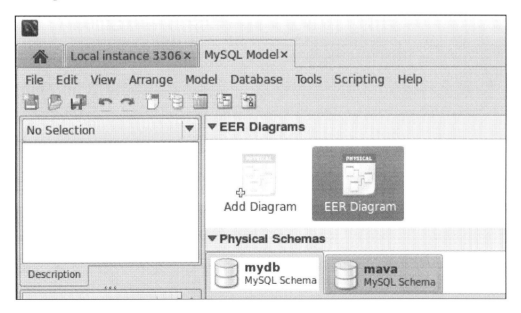

4. If you open the diagram, the only table (**User**) in our project will be displayed. We created this in *Chapter 2, The Request and Response Life Cycle*, for testing purposes.

Adding a new entity

As I mentioned before, each table that we create here will represent an entity in our Symfony project. To build one, let's start with the `workcpace` table:

1. Press *T*, click on any empty space on the canvas, and double-click on the newly created entity (table) to change its name to `workcpace`, as follows:

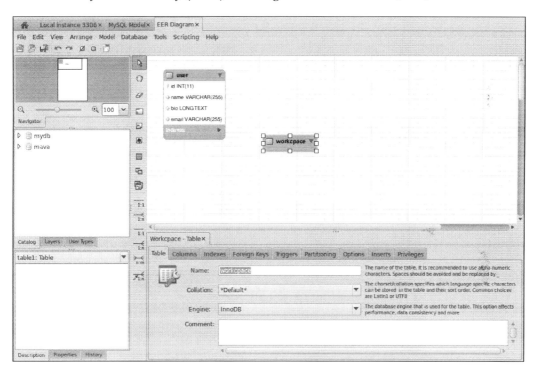

2. Click on the **Columns** tab, and first create an `id` column and set the **PK** (Primary Key), **NN** (Not Null), and **AI** (Auto-increment) options for it. Then, add the rest of the properties as follows (You can add columns by double-clicking on the empty line beneath the last added column.):

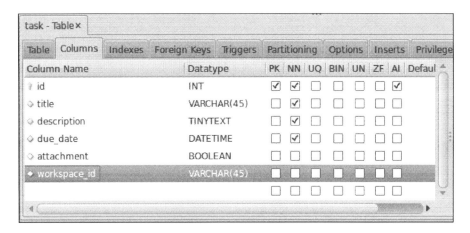

You might expect more columns in the `task` table. For the sake of simplicity, let's start small and add a more complex structure if it is needed later.

 You can change the name and datatype for each column by double-clicking on it.

The navigation area in the top left-hand side of the window helps you zoom and drag the preview area wherever you like.

Use the facts from the previous chapter and repeat the same process for other entities. At the end, you should have a structure as follows:

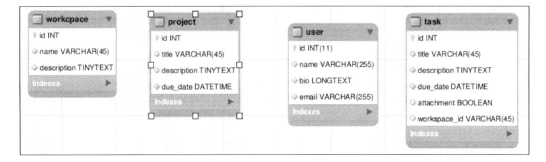

Adding a new relationship

In terms of relationships, we had three rules:

- Each project can be defined in one workspace only but each workspace can have multiple projects. This means that there is a one-to-many relationship between workspace and project.

- Each task belongs to one project only but each project may contain multiple tasks. Here is another one-to-many relationship, this time, between project and task.

- Each task can be assigned to one user only but each user can have multiple tasks. Again, we have a one-to-many relationship between user and task.

It looks like we have a couple of one-to-many relationships between entities. To implement any of these relationships, we need to create a column for the foreign key first, then connect it to the referenced column of the other table. For the Workspace-Project relationship, for example, do the following:

1. Click on the **project** entity and add a new column called `workspace_id` to it. For datatype, consider `INT`.

2. Now click on the **Foreign Keys** tab and add a new key named `fk_project`. Under the **Referenced Table**, add `mava`.`workcpace`. Then, in the **Foreign Key Columns** section, connect `workspace_id` to `id` by checking the box. By doing this, you will see that a dashed line connects these two entities in the preview pane:

The rest of the relationships are one-to-many as well, so after repeating the same process, you should have an ERD as follows:

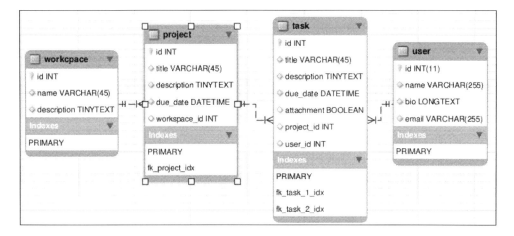

This is far from complete, but for MVP purposes, it does the job. We just created a visual concept of our entities, their properties, and relationships with each other. Seeing how the business logic looks like—at any stage of development—helps understand it better and prevent some ordinary mistakes. Let's see how to use it to create actual tables in the database and real entities in Symfony.

Creating actual tables from a diagram

Creating tables from an ERD is called Forward Engineering and includes the following steps:

1. Select **Database | Forward Engineer** (*Ctrl + G*) and connect to the host where you set up the mava database then press **Next**:

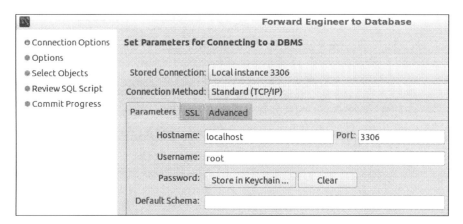

2. In the **Options** step, make sure that you drop any current tables before creating new ones. Accept the default state of other options (leave them unchecked) and press **Next**:

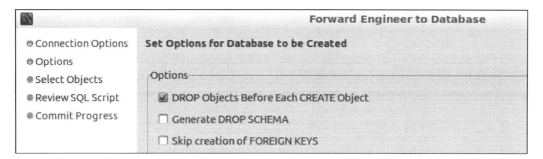

3. This step might ask for your password. After authorization, make sure that only Table objects are selected:

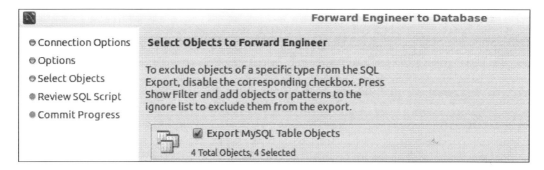

4. This step shows you a preview of a SQL query containing all four table creations and their related configurations. It is not necessary, but if you wish, you can copy this script to the clipboard in case you need it somewhere:

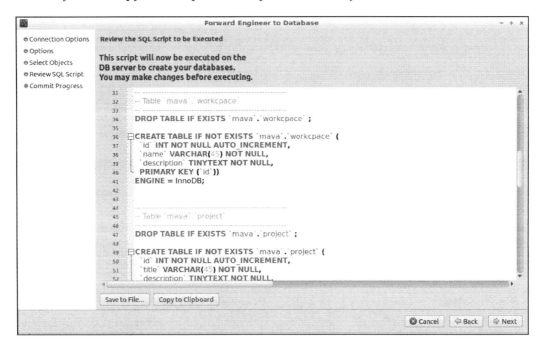

5. By pressing **Next**, all steps are processed and the tables are created:

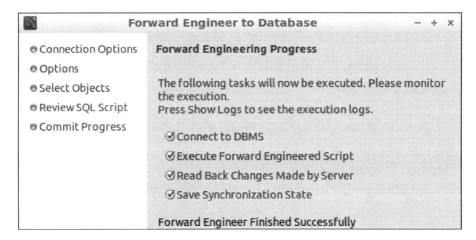

You can confirm that new tables were created by going to your host, choosing the mava database, and refreshing the list of tables.

Generating entities

Now, let's ask Symfony to do the last step and generate entities. The following command investigates the database and creates a group of configuration files (in the .yml format):

```
$ bin/console doctrine:mapping:import --force AppBundle yml
```

If everything is okay, you should see this output:

```
Importing mapping information from "default" entity manager
  > writing /var/www/packt/mava/src/AppBundle/Resources/config/doctrine/Project.orm.yml
  > writing /var/www/packt/mava/src/AppBundle/Resources/config/doctrine/Task.orm.yml
  > writing /var/www/packt/mava/src/AppBundle/Resources/config/doctrine/User.orm.yml
  > writing /var/www/packt/mava/src/AppBundle/Resources/config/doctrine/Workspace.orm.yml
```

Open any of these .orm.yml files and you will find all columns, keys, and relationships defined here. Now we can use these files to create entities. First, you need to get rid of the already defined /Entity/User.php entity. It conflicts with the definitions in config files. After deleting this file, turn the YML file into an annotation by running the following:

```
$ bin/console doctrine:mapping:convert annotation ./src
```

The output says that every config file has been processed and an annotated entity has been generated for them:

```
Processing entity "AppBundle\Entity\User"
Processing entity "AppBundle\Entity\Task"
Processing entity "AppBundle\Entity\Project"
Processing entity "AppBundle\Entity\Workspace"

Exporting "annotation" mapping information to "/var/www/packt/mava/src"
```

Now, it is safe to completely remove the /AppBundle/Resources/config/doctrine folder and all .orm.yml files in it.

Check your /Entity folder and there you have all the entity files created. However, something is missing. Look in any of them and you will find that there are no set() or get() methods. Besides, there are no repositories. To fix this, first open each file and edit the @ORM\Entity annotation as follows (This line is normally located at the top of the page, line 11.):

```
@ORM\Entity(repositoryClass="AppBundle\Entity\UserRepository")
```

Repeat this process for each entity and then run this command:

```
$ bin/console doctrine:generate:entities AppBundle
```

This will add all the missing pieces to our entities and generate their repositories.

Data fixtures

To play with these newly created entities, we need to add some data fixtures. Let's say we need one workspace, one project, and three tasks, one of them assigned to John and the other two assigned to Jack. (Remember these two guys from the previous data fixtures? Just open `src/AppBundle/DataFixtures/ORM/LoadUsers.php` to remind yourself about a little bit of history from *Chapter 2, The Request and Response Life Cycle*.)

Create a new data fixture for workspace and add the following contents to it:

```php
<?php
// src/AppBundle/DataFixtures/ORM/LoadWorkspaces.php
namespace AppBundle\DataFixtures\ORM;
use Doctrine\Common\Persistence\ObjectManager;
use Doctrine\Common\DataFixtures\AbstractFixture;
use Doctrine\Common\DataFixtures\OrderedFixtureInterface;
use AppBundle\Entity\Workspace;

class LoadWorkspaces extends AbstractFixture implements
  OrderedFixtureInterface
{
  public function load(ObjectManager $manager)
  {
    $workspace1 = new Workspace();
    $workspace1->setName('Writing');
    $workspace1->setDescription('info for writing Workspace');
    $manager->persist($workspace1);
    $manager->flush();
    $this->addReference('workspace-writing', $workspace1);
  }

  public function getOrder()
  {
    return 10; // the order in which fixtures will be loaded
  }
}
```

In this code, there are two major things that we need to focus on. First, the `addReference()` method, which basically creates a reference that we will use to make a connection between a workspace and its projects. We can use this method because our class has implemented `OrderedFixtureInterface`.

The other important method is `getOrder()`. Basically, you define the order of loading fixtures and it comes in handy in a situation where the contents of one entity somehow depend on the contents of the other one.

 Use `getOrder()` with a return value of 20, 30, and 40 for `LoadProjects`, `LoadUsers`, and `LoadTasks` respectively. It is a good practice to have a gap of 10 units, in case later on we need to add another file in between.

So let's see how we can use the workspace reference in the `LoadProjects` fixture:

```php
<?php
// src/AppBundle/DataFixtures/ORM/LoadProjects.php
// ...
use AppBundle\Entity\Project;

class LoadProjects extends AbstractFixture implements
  OrderedFixtureInterface
{
  public function load(ObjectManager $manager)
  {
    $project1 = new Project();
    $project1->setTitle('Symfony book');
    $project1->setDescription('Some descriptions for Symfony book
      project');
    $project1->setDueDate(new \DateTime('2014-10-20'));
    $project1->setWorkspace($manager->merge($this-
      >getReference('workspace-writing')));
    $manager->persist($project1);
    $manager->flush();
    $this->addReference('project-symfony', $project1);
  }
// getOrder() method
}
```

Pay close attention to the `setWorkspace()` method. It gets `ObjectManager` to fetch the reference to the workspace and assign it to the `workspace_id` field in the current project entity.

Moreover, there is a call to the `addReference()` method for the project entity because we need to use it for tasks. Speaking about tasks, this is how the fixture would look:

```php
<?php
// src/AppBundle/DataFixtures/ORM/LoadTasks.php
// ...
use AppBundle\Entity\Task;

class LoadTasks extends AbstractFixture implements
  OrderedFixtureInterface
{
  public function load(ObjectManager $manager)
  {
    $task1 = new Task();
    $task1->setTitle('writing chapter 1');
    $task1->setDescription('descriptions for writing ch1');
    $task1->setDueDate(new \DateTime('2014-10-14'));
    $task1->setProject($manager->merge($this-
      >getReference('project-symfony')));
    $task1->setUser($manager->merge($this->getReference('user-
      john')));

    $task2 = new Task();
    $task2->setTitle('reviewing chapter 1');
    $task2->setDescription('descriptions for reviewing ch1');
    $task2->setDueDate(new \DateTime('2014-10-16'));
    $task2->setProject($manager->merge($this-
      >getReference('project-symfony')));
    $task2->setUser($manager->merge($this->getReference('user-
      jack')));

    $task3 = new Task();
    $task3->setTitle('editing chapter 1');
    $task3->setDescription('descriptions for editing ch1');
    $task3->setDueDate(new \DateTime('2014-10-18'));
    $task3->setProject($manager->merge($this-
      >getReference('project-symfony')));
    $task3->setUser($manager->merge($this->getReference('user-
      jack')));

    $manager->persist($task1);
    $manager->persist($task2);
    $manager->persist($task3);
    $manager->flush();
  }
  // getOrder() method
}
```

There are two reference calls in any task entity. First, there is a call to the project that the current task belongs to and then there is a call to the user to whom this task has been assigned. The last fixture that we need to load (or basically edit) is user. Open the file and update the contents as follows:

```php
<?php
// src/AppBundle/DataFixtures/ORM/LoadUsers.php
// ...
use AppeBundle\Entity\User;

class LoadUsers extends AbstractFixture implements
  OrderedFixtureInterface
{
  public function load(ObjectManager $manager)
  {
    // previous code
    $this->addReference('user-john', $user1);
    $this->addReference('user-jack', $user2);
  }

  // getOrder() method
}
```

Okay, all data fixtures are in place, and now it is time to load them to tables:

```
$ bin/console doctrine:fixtures:load
```

Answer *Y* to the purging database question and, after that, check any table (task table, for example) to see how data is loaded and related to each other:

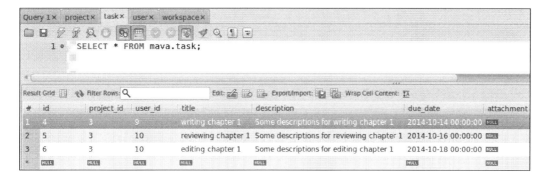

With the entities created and fixtures loaded, I think this is a good time to add all of these files to our GitHub repository:

```
$ git commit -am "chapter 5 - entities and datafixtures added"
$ git push
```

 As Jenkins picks up new changes from GitHub automatically, you might receive a notification regarding a failed or successful build. Ignore the e-mail either way. We will deal with it later.

Now we are all set and ready to create some scenarios around the business logic and implement each feature.

Some business logic features and scenarios

Generally speaking, we expect four main actions (CRUD: Create Read Update Delete) for each entity. Although they can be generated by Doctrine automatically (via Symfony's `bin/console doctrine:generate:crud` command), we will see in *Chapter 6*, *Dashboard and Security*, how to use the Sonata project (`https://sonata-project.org/`) to do the job for us. So there won't be any features for them at the moment. Instead, let's focus on a search feature and various scenarios around it.

As this is a task management application, all searches will be built around the task entity. Yes, we will have features to list, sort, and quick-search users, projects, and workspaces on their own page. However, the search box on the main page should be focused mainly on tasks. Let's see what search possibilities we can imagine for it.

Basically, we need a search box that accepts search keywords and then performs searches on various entities. It is easy to look for the title and description of a task, but we need a more robust search mechanism.

For example, if the keyword is a date, it should be able to look in the `due_date` field for each task and return them in case there is a match.

If it is a username, then it should be able to find all tasks assigned to a specific username. This means that the search criteria should be expanded to the user entity via the relationship between the task and user.

How about a project name? If we mention a project title as a search keyword, it should be able to find all tasks belonging to that project.

So technically the task search mechanism should be smart enough to perform the following:

1. First, analyze the search keyword and decide an appropriate data type for it.
2. Then, decide the searching criteria for it (whether it is in the task entity or outside it, considering the task entity has the highest priority).
3. Finally, perform the search query and return the results.

Searching tasks is one of the most important pieces of business logic in this project and, as you will see, more assumptions (search filters and parameters) will be added to it.

TDD and BDD with Codeception

Now is a good opportunity to see Codeception and our understanding of TDD and BDD in action. To implement a maintainable code, we are going to follow these three steps:

1. First, we create a failing functional test (a scenario) that summarizes our expectations of the application. This means that according to the business logic, we need to see an overall function related to each entity. So we will create actions that, without worrying about what they will have inside, simply return a desired response.
2. Next, we create a failing unit test and assess the legitimacy of the response created from step one. In other words, we test the logic in each action to make sure that the generated response is accurate.
3. Finally, we create acceptance tests to see if the tests created from the first two steps satisfy the application performance from the end user's point of view. In this step, we see the results in a browser, and we can see how our application interacts with JavaScript codes or Ajax calls.

Step one – creating a functional test

Earlier in this chapter, we created data fixtures for all four entities of our project. To be specific, we have at least one workspace called `Writing` that has a project named `Symfony book` with three tasks that are assigned to two users. The general picture of this scenario is as follows:

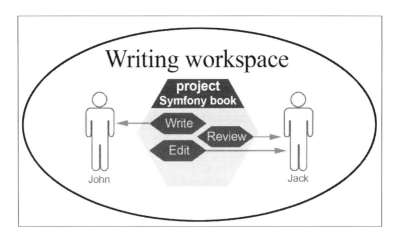

Let's start with the workspace and ask Codeception to create a functional test for it:

```
$ vendor/bin/codecept generate:cest functional WorkspaceController
```

Great, we just created a class-based functional test (`cest`) for our `WorkspaceController` (which does not exist yet):

Test was created in /var/www/packt/mava/tests/functional/ WorkspaceControllerCest.php

Now, let's open the new test file and add the following scenario to it:

```php
// mava/tests/functional/WorkspaceControllerCest.php
<?php
class WorkspaceControllerCest
{
  // ...
  public function testShowAction(FunctionalTester $I)
  {
    $I->wantTo('too see inside the \"Writing\" workspace');
    $I->amOnPage('/workspace/writing');
    $I->see('Symfony book');
  }
}
```

We know it is a failing test, and to prove it, we can run it and check the output:

```
$ vendor/bin/codecept run functional WorkspaceControlerCest
```

We can spot a few facts from this scenario:

- We need a controller called: `WorkspaceController`
- We need a `showAction()` method there
- This method receives a workspace name as input and renders a template where a list of available projects for this workspace is displayed

Developing the missing code

Starting from the missing controller and its `showAction()`, go to `AppBundle` and add the following class to it:

```php
// mava/src/AppBundle/Controller/WorkspaceController.php
<?php
namespace AppBundle\Controller;
use Sensio\Bundle\FrameworkExtraBundle\Configuration\Route;
use Symfony\Bundle\FrameworkBundle\Controller\Controller;
use Symfony\Component\HttpFoundation\Response;

class WorkspaceController extends Controller
{
  /**
   * @Route("/workspace/{name}", name="workspace_show")
   * @param $name
   * @return Response
   */
  public function showAction($name)
  {
    // ToDo:find available projects in the given workspace
    return $this->render('workspace/show.html.twig',
      array('project' => 'Symfony book'));
  }
}
```

The key points in the new controller are: we have a new route (`/workspace/{name}`) and a new template, which lives in the `app/Resources/views` folder and is called `show.html.twig`.

As you can see, this template gets a `project` object and will show the name of the project later. From a functional test point of view, what matters is getting a response and rendering it. So for now, it doesn't matter how this project object was obtained. We will deal with it shortly. Just put the project name `Symfony book` in it and pass it on to the template.

Now we need to create the template. Go to the `app/Resources/views` folder and create the missing `workspace` subdirectory and its template as follows:

```
# mava/app/Resources/views/workspace/show.twig.html
{{ project }}
```

Nothing fancy here. We just display what we get from the `showAction()` controller. Now it is time to run the test:

```
$ vendor/bin/codecept generate:cest functional WorkspaceController
```

The test now passes beautifully:

```
Functional Tests (1) ------------------------------------------------

Too see inside the "writing" workspace (WorkspaceControllerCest::testShow
Action) Ok

--------------------------------------------------------------

Time: 523 ms, Memory: 29.00Mb

OK (1 test, 1 assertion)
```

Step two – creating the unit tests

With the initial functional test in place, let's deal with the unit tests and get rid of comments and fake responses in the `showAction()` method. First, let's ask Codeception to generate the unit test file for us:

```
$ vendor/bin/codecept generate:test unit WorkspaceController
```

```
Test was created in /var/www/packt/mava/tests/unit/
WorkspaceControllerTest.php
```

This was easy, but here comes the tricky part. The nature of the `showAction()` method suggests some interaction with the database. In other words, we have to interact with two entities. We have a name property for a workspace entity, with this workspace name we need to check the project entity and find all projects that belong to the given workspace.

Setting up the database for a test environment in the right way

The first thing that we need to do is isolate the development (or production) database from our test code. So, let's modify parameters and configuration files for the test environment to implement this isolation.

Open the `parameters.yml` file and add the following lines to it:

```
# mava/app/config/parameters.yml
parameters:
  database_name_test: mava_test
  #...
```

Now open the `config_test.yml` file and add the following lines to it:

```
# mava/app/config/config_test.yml
doctrine:
  dbal:
    dbname:    "%database_name_test%"
```

Now we use Doctrine to create the new test database, add tables to it, and populate the tables with sample data:

```
$ bin/console doctrine:database:create --env=test
Created database `mava_test` for connection named default


$ bin/console doctrine:schema:update --env=test --force
Updating database schema...
Database schema updated successfully! "7" queries were executed


$ bin/console doctrine:fixtures:load --env=test
Careful, database will be purged. Do you want to continue y/N ?y
  > purging database
  > loading [10] AppBundle\DataFixtures\ORM\LoadWorkspaces
  > loading [20] AppBundle\DataFixtures\ORM\LoadProjects
  > loading [30] AppBundle\DataFixtures\ORM\LoadUsers
  > loading [40] AppBundle\DataFixtures\ORM\LoadTasks
```

Notice the --env=test option in the preceding commands. If you forget it, the main database and its tables will be affected. With the --env=test option, we tell Doctrine which environment we want to work on.

Dropping and recreating the database for each test

In a proper test procedure, we should be able to drop the tables, recreate them, and populate them with fresh data in each test. Codeception can handle this masterfully. Look at the tests/_data/ folder and you will find an empty file called dump.sql. All we need to do is add some SQL commands to create and populate tables here. In MySQL Workbench, it is in the **Management** tab under the **Data Export** option.

In **PhpMyAdmin**, you can select the mava_test database and then choose **Export**.

Either way, save the file with the dump.sql name and move it to mava/tests/_data/dump.sql.

Next, go to the codeception.yml file at the root of your project and modify the Db settings as follows:

```
# mava/codeception.yml
modules:
  config:
    Db:
      dsn: 'mysql:host=localhost; dbname=mava_test'
      user: 'root'
      password: 'illuminati'
      dump: tests/_data/dump.sql
      populate: true # dump will be loaded before the test
      cleanup: false  # dump will be loaded after each test
```

Then, enable the Db module in the unit test suit as follows:

```
# mava/tests/unit.suit.yml
class_name: UnitTester
modules:
  enabled:
    - Asserts
    - \Helper\Unit
    - Db
```

To see if the tables are created and populated in each test, drop the database, run the empty test (it will pass because there is nothing to test yet), and check the tables:

```
$ vendor/bin/codecept run unit WorkspaceControllerTest

Unit Tests (1) ----------------------------------------------------

Test show action (WorkspaceControllerTest::testShowAction)      Ok

-------------------------------------------------------------------

Time: 569 ms, Memory: 10.00Mb

OK (1 test, 0 assertions)
```

You will see that the database, tables, and their records are all there.

Now, let's add the `Doctrine2` module to `unit.suite.yml` and get ready to write the first unit test:

```
# mava/tests/unit.suite.yml
class_name: UnitTester
modules:
  enabled:
    - Asserts
    - \Helper\Unit
    - Db
    - Symfony2:
      app_path: 'app'
      var_path: 'var'
      environment: 'test'
    - Doctrine2:
      depends: Symfony2
```

In the preceding settings, we declare that the Doctrine2 module should use the default Entity Manager available in the Symfony2 module.

Creating unit tests

Now that we have all the Db settings in order, let's write the first test. We can do this by checking the name of the project. In other words, let's see if a project named `Symfony book` is available in the `Writing` workspace. Basically, we are going to test the repository first. So open the recently created unit test file and modify it as follows:

```
// mava/tests/unit/WorkspaceControllerTest.php
<?php
class WorkspaceControllerTest extends \Codeception\TestCase\Test
{
  /**
```

```
   * @var \UnitTester
   */
  protected $tester;
  // ...
  public function testShowAction()
  {
    $workspaceId  = $this->tester->grabFromRepository(
      'AppBundle:Workspace', 'id',
      array('name'=>'Writing')
    );
    $projectTitle = $this->tester->grabFromRepository(
      'AppBundle:Project', 'title',
      array('workspace'=>$workspaceId)
    );
    $this->assertEquals('Symfony book', $projectTitle, 'no match
      found');
  }
}
```

Run the test and you will see that it passes successfully. However, this test is not good enough. We didn't actually test our controller. We just checked the repositories. To test the controller, we first need to get rid of the hardcoded value in the `showAction()` method that we passed to the template. This value is supposed to be generated by controller. So replace it with a variable as follows:

```
// mava/src/AppBundle/Controller/WorkspaceController.php
<?php
// ...
class WorkspaceController extends Controller
{
  // ...
  public function showAction($name)
  {
    // ToDO: find workspace projects via given workspace name
    return $this->render('workspace/show.html.twig',
      array('projects' => $projects));
  }
}
```

Now open the `helper` class for unit tests and add a new method to it:

```
// mava/tests/_support/helper/Unit.php
<?php
namespace Helper;
class Unit extends \Codeception\Module
{
```

```
public function seeResponseContains($text)
{
  $this->assertContains(
    $text,
    $this->getModule('Symfony2')->_getResponseContent(),
    "response contains"
  );
}
}
```

This method simply checks to see whether a given text is available in Symfony's response object.

 We could define the new `helper` method directly in our unit test class. However, keeping helpers organized in the `Helper` class keeps our code clean and maintainable.

Now add the following lines at the end of the test file:

```
// mava/tests/unit/WorkspaceControllerTest.php
<?php
class WorkspaceControllerTest extends \Codeception\TestCase\Test
{
  /**
   * @var \UnitTester
   */
  protected $tester;
// ...
  public function testShowAction()
  {
    // ...
    $this->tester->amOnRoute('workspace_show', array('name' =>
      'Writing'));
    $this->tester->seeResponseContains('Symfony book');
  }
}
```

The `amOnRoute()` method gets the route name to `showAction()` and passes `Writing` as the workspace name. Then, using the new helper `seeResponseContains()` method, we look for our project name, `Symfony book`.

Now we have a unit test that actually tests the repository plus our controller. Run the test:

```
Unit Tests (1)---------------------------------------------------------
Test show action (WorkspaceControllerTest::testShowAction)        Fail
-----------------------------------------------------------------------
Time: 739 ms, Memory: 31.75Mb


There was 1 failure:
---------

1) Test show action (WorkspaceControllerTest::testShowAction)
response contains
Failed asserting that '$project' contains "Symfony book".
FAILURES!
Tests: 1, Assertions: 2, Failures: 1.
```

This is great. This means that our mission is to write a code to pass the test. Luckily, we know the cause for failing as well. The output clearly says that it couldn't find the Symfony book string in the $project variable. This makes our job really easy.

Writing the code to pass the test

The showAction() method will find projects based on a given workspace name. To do so, we first have to find out the workspace ID and use it to find available projects:

```php
// mava/src/AppBundle/Controller/WorkspaceController.php
<?php
// ...
class WorkspaceController extends Controller
{
  /...
  public function showAction($name)
  {
    // find the workspace id from the given name
    $repo = $this->getDoctrine()
      ->getRepository('AppBundle:Workspace');
    $workspace = $repo->findOneBy(array('name' => $name));
    $workspaceId = $workspace->getId();

    // find all projects which have the given workspace id
    $repo = $this->getDoctrine()
      ->getRepository('AppBundle:Project');
    $projects = $repo->findBy(
      array('workspace' => $workspaceId)
```

```
    );

    if ($projects == null) {
      throw $this->createNotFoundException('Not found!' );
    }
    else
      return $this->render(
        'workspace/show.html.twig',
        array('projects' => $projects)
      );
  }
}
```

You might have noticed that we are not sending a simple string to the template, rather we are sending an array of objects ($projects). This means that we have to modify our template accordingly to handle this change:

```
# mava/app/Resources/views/workspace/show.twig.html
{% for project in projects %}
  {{ project.title }}
{% endfor %}
```

In the preceding template, we simply loop through all the available projects, fetch the project title, and print it on the screen. The {{ }} and {% %} symbols belong to TWIG and we will talk about this in detail in *Chapter 7, The Presentation Layer*.

Running functional and unit tests

Now let's run all the tests that we have created so far and check the results:

```
$ vendor/bin/codecept run


Unit Tests (1) ----------------------------------------------------
Test show action (WorkspaceControllerTest::testShowAction)          Ok


Functional Tests (1) ----------------------------------------------
Too see inside the "writing" workspace (WorkspaceControllerCest::testShow
Action)                        Ok


Acceptance Tests (0) ------------------------
---------------------------------------------
Time: 805 ms, Memory: 35.25Mb
OK (2 tests, 3 assertions)
```

As the output suggests, we have two passing (unit and functional) tests with a total of three assertions. Now we have one more test to do and that is the acceptance test.

Step three – creating an acceptance test

No testing procedure is complete without an acceptance test. As developers, we tend to focus on the codes and dark screens to the extent that we sometimes forget the user experience. How do you know that the code you have created is good enough to solve a problem if you can't get feedback from the user's point of view?

With an acceptance test (that is, **User Acceptance Test (UAT)**), we can see how our application performs in the real world.

Head to your terminal and create a new classified acceptance test:

```
$ vendor/bin/codecept g:cest acceptance WorkspaceControllerAccept
Test was created in var/www/packt/mava/tests/acceptance/
WorkspaceControllerAcceptCest.php
```

Now, run Selenium2, which you installed in *Chapter 4, Using Behavior-Driven Development in Symfony*, and get ready to see it taking control of the automated test:

```
$ java -jar path/to/selenium-server.jar
```

To see the result on the screen, we need to configure `acceptance.suite.yml` to open a real browser while testing:

```
# mava/tests/acceptance.suite.yml
class_name: AcceptanceTester
modules:
  enabled:
    - WebDriver:
      url: http://localhost:8000
      browser: firefox
#    - PhpBrowser:
#      url: http://localhost:8000
    - \Helper\Acceptance
```

 Keep `PhpBrowser` commented out in the `acceptance.suite.yml` file. You might need it later for a faster acceptance test.

Next, open the new acceptance test file and add the following commands to it:

```
// mava/tests/acceptance/WorkspaceControllerAcceptCest.php
<?php
class WorkspaceControllerAcceptCest
{
  // ...
  public function testShowAction(AcceptanceTester $I)
  {
    $I->wantTo('too see inside the "Writing" workspace');
    $I->amOnPage('/workspace/writing');
    $I->see('Symfony book');
    $I->wait(3);
  }
}
```

Hang on a minute! This is almost the same test that we created for the functional test, isn't it? That's correct. The fact is acceptance and functional tests are mostly identical and the only differences are as follows:

- Acceptance tests can be run in a browser
- They can cover JavaScript calls as well

 The $I->wait(3); method delays the closing of the Firefox browser for three seconds so that we get a chance to see the output.

Now let's run all the tests and see how it looks:

```
$ vendor/bin/codecept run


Codeception PHP Testing Framework v2.1.5
Powered by PHPUnit 4.8.22 by Sebastian Bergmann and contributors.


Unit Tests (1) ---------------------------------------------------------
Test show action (WorkspaceControllerTest::testShowAction)         Ok
------------------------------------------------------------------------


Functional Tests (1) ---------------------------------------------------
Too see inside the "writing" workspace (WorkspaceControllerCest::testShow
Action)                         Ok
```

```
-------------------------------------------------------------------


Acceptance Tests (1) --------------------------------------------------
Too see inside the "writing" workspace (WorkspaceControllerAcceptCest::te
stShowAction)                        Ok

-------------------------------------------------------------------



Time: 6.21 seconds, Memory: 35.25Mb

OK (3 tests, 4 assertions)
```

Congratulations. There are three tests and four assertions and they are all green. As you saw in the UAT step, a Firefox browser opened and browsed to the Writing workspace, the Symfony book contents were displayed, and the browser was closed after three seconds.

> In case your internal PHP server was terminated since the last time, make sure that it is up and running before executing the tests:
> ```
> $ bin/console server:run
> ```

On the CI side of the story

Last time, as you pushed the changes to your GitHub repository, you probably received a couple of e-mails informing you about the success or failure of the new build. You can celebrate if your build is successful. However, if it is not, don't panic and just follow this two-step process.

First, make sure that all unit tests and functional tests in your local machine pass successfully. If there is something wrong here, you should not expect a successful build from your Jenkins instance on EC2. For those who created or modified the tests and codes themselves, it could be a simple misspelling error or some serious logical issue. Spot the problem using log messages and fix it. Then try again.

For those who cloned the code from my GitHub repository, it could be a local configuration issue. If you branched out your working Git repository, make sure that you are on the right branch. If something needed to be merged, check out to your Dev branch first and then do it. Check that the phpunit.xml file is in the right place. Make sure that you have set permissions correctly.

If locally everything is okay, then the problem is in your Jenkins server. Before doing anything, read the log files. They are very direct and lead you exactly to the root of the problem.

 Sometimes, upgrading the installed plugins in Jenkins fixes the problems automatically.

Summary

In this chapter, we built a tiny business logic around four entities provided so far and created unit, functional, and acceptance tests for their controllers and repositories.

Don't worry if it looks very simple at the moment. Remember that we are still dealing with an MVP. We are waiting for two more players in this project. In other words, in the next chapter, the security and administrative areas will be added to the project, and in *Chapter 7, The Presentation Layer*, the main focus will be on the frontend and making the project look pretty. Then, in *Chapter 8, Project Review*, we will go completely crazy and make all the mechanisms used so far five times bigger and more complex. That's where all the features expected from a big project will be applied to the mava project.

6
Dashboard and Security

It is nice to have entities and business logic in place. What would be nicer is having a control panel where we can **Create,Read,Update, and Delete (CRUD)** them and make sure that only specific users with the right privileges can have access to it. This sounds like a firewalled and secured area of the project.

In this chapter, we will see how to set up security and firewalls in Symfony, and then create a user management system using `FOSUserBundle`. After knowing the basics, we step into one of the biggest Symfony projects, Sonata, and use some of its bundles. We will see how to use `SonataAdminBundle` to manage entities from the backend. However, as an account owner (not administrator), we need to be able to manage our workspaces, projects, tasks, and members from the frontend as well. This means that we need to set up at least two firewalls for this project. One will be built in the frontend where every member keeps his own stuff, and one will be set for the backend where only the website administrators have access.

The main topics in this chapter are as follows:

- Setting up a firewall and defining authentication and authorization steps
- Using FOSUserBundle for better user management on the frontend
- Using SonataAdminBundle for better content management on the backend:

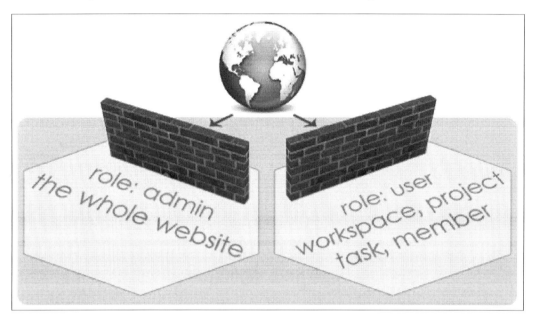

Using SonataUserBundle to integrate the user entity into the backend

How security is organized in Symfony?

Security is all about defining an agreement between users and the application on how to use the website. Like other Symfony configuration files, security has its own settings, which basically define what type of user is allowed to visit which part of the application and types of operations that he is authorized to do. If you look at `app/config/security.yml` contents, it is quite empty and security is deactivated by default. This is the reason that you can see almost any part of your application without providing any credentials. Let's change this and build some firewalls in front of locations such as `/admin`.

Creating a firewall is as simple as adding the following lines to the `security.yml` contents:

```
# app/config/security.yml
security:
    firewalls:
```

```
        secured_area:
            pattern:    ^/
            anonymous: ~

    access_control:
        - { path: ^/admin/, roles: ROLE_ADMIN }
```

This URL is now secured from unauthorized access. However, it is not going to be isolated forever. In other words, we need to find a way to let the genuine users come in. This happens through a mechanism called authentication.

Authentication

Authentication is the process that determines who the user is. During this process, a key (called token) is given to the user, which lets them pass through the first security barrier. The detailed process is something like this.

First, the firewall looks inside the request and fetches the credentials (that is, the username and password) and creates an unauthenticated token. There is a class inside Symfony's Security component called UsernamePasswordToken that is in charge of doing this:

```
use Symfony\Component\Security\Core\Authentication\Token\
UsernamePasswordToken;
// . . .
$unauthenticatedToken = new UsernamePasswordToken(
            $username,
            $password,
            $this->providerKey
        );
```

The providerKey here can come from a third-party application or it could be generated by Symfony itself. As you can see, it simply says: Yes, I got the request, and yes, there are some credentials in it. So, here is your unauthenticated token, but I still don't know you, dude."

The next step would be checking the credentials to see whether they are correct. If so, then another method will convert the current token to an authenticated one:

```
use Symfony\Component\Security\Core\Authentication\
AuthenticationManagerInterface;
$authenticatedToken = $this
            ->authenticationManager
            ->authenticate($unauthenticatedToken);
```

So, at this stage, we got the authenticated token and passed through the firewall safely. To have this token handy at all times, it should be saved in a concept called security context:

```
/**
 * @var SecurityContextInterface
 */
private $securityContext;

$this->container->get('security.token_storage')->setToken($token);
```

This way, we can retrieve the token whenever it is needed.

Authorization

The first security barrier is passed and imagine that we are in /admin/workspace now. What happens if we decided to remove a workspace?

In general, there are many parameters involved in authorization but technically everything comes down to one important question. The Security component will ask: "Are you authorized to do that?" This authorization decision is usually made based on the current token in the security context:

```
if (!$securityContext->isGranted('ROLE_ADMIN')) {
    throw new AccessDeniedException();
}
```

This sounds like a lot of effort is involved in implementing a good security system for Symfony projects. Taking care of all of those firewalls and authentication and authorization steps is definitely a delicate and important task. However, the good news is that there are some bundles out there that have already implemented the security requirements. Let's see how to benefit from them in this chapter.

Handling users with FOSUserBundle

This is the best user management bundle so far. It comes with many user management features (such as user registration, edit profile, forgotten password, and others) out of the box. All you need to do is install and activate the bundle and extend your own User entity from it. Let's start with the installation:

```
$ composer require friendsofsymfony/user-bundle '~dev-master'
```

At the time of writing this chapter, there are some unresolved issues between Symfony 3 and stable releases of `FOSUserBundle` that are being fixed on a daily basis. So, if you don't see any stable version greater than or equal to v2.0, make sure that you are using the master branch.

Of course, then we need to activate it:

```php
<?php
// app/AppKernel.php
public function registerBundles()
{
    $bundles = array(
        // ...
        new FOS\UserBundle\FOSUserBundle(),
    );
}
```

Now we need to modify the current User entity and extend it from this bundle. Get rid of the e-mail, name, and bio and their setters and getters as we don't need them anymore and there are more robust fields already created in `FOSUserBundle` entities:

```php
<?php
// src/AppBundle/Entity/User.php
namespace AppBundle\Entity;
use FOS\UserBundle\Model\User as BaseUser;
use Doctrine\ORM\Mapping as ORM;

class User extends BaseUser
{
protected $id;
    public function __construct()
    {
        parent::__construct();
        // your own logic
    }
}
```

Note that $id is defined as protected and a constructor has been initiated from the parent class because there are lots of features that we can use this way.

Additionally, look at the FOS's User class. It is inside the Model folder that we talked about in the previous chapter. This means that it is equipped with extra methods that we can benefit from, without adding them directly to our own User entity. All we need to do is just call them.

Security settings

With the bundle installed and the User entity extended from it, we can now define our security rules. Open `app/config/security.yml` and add the following contents to it:

```
# app/config/security.yml
security:
    providers:
        fos_userbundle:
            id: fos_user.user_provider.username
    encoders:

        FOS\UserBundle\Model\UserInterface: bcrypt
    role_hierarchy:
        ROLE_ADMIN:        ROLE_USER
        ROLE_SUPER_ADMIN: ROLE_ADMIN
    firewalls:
        main:
            pattern: ^/
            form_login:
                provider: fos_userbundle

                csrf_token_generator: security.csrf.token_manager
            logout:        true
            anonymous:     true
    access_control:
        - { path: ^/login$, role: IS_AUTHENTICATED_ANONYMOUSLY }
        - { path: ^/register, role: IS_AUTHENTICATED_ANONYMOUSLY }
        - { path: ^/resetting, role: IS_AUTHENTICATED_ANONYMOUSLY}
            - { path: ^/admin/, role: ROLE_ADMIN }
```

Here is a description of each entry:

- With encoders, you can set the User entity and encryption algorithm that is used for passwords. As you can see, we have bcrypt here.

- The `role_hierarchy` entry defines who controls who. So `ROLE_ADMIN:` `ROLE_USER` basically means that whichever permission is granted to a user is contained in admin as well.

- With the provider, you can define an alias for the service provider and access this alias conveniently whenever it is needed. Basically, a provider is responsible for retrieving the user details. If you look at the default security settings—before replacing them with the preceding configurations—you can see that the 'provider' key was set to the 'in-memory' value. This means that no matter how the user has been stored, whether it is hardcoded into a file (that is, in-memory) or provided by a database (that is, FOSUserBundle's User model), the provider's job is providing the user's details.

- The most important part is the firewall, where you define areas of your application that need to be secured. In this example, we set that an anonymous user can visit anywhere, but don't be confused, because of the `access_control` entry, they can only log in, register, and password reset pages, which makes sense. We will make some changes to the `security.yml` file as we continue.

Adding the required configurations to FOSUserBundle

The next step is defining the settings for the `config.yml` file, such as defining registration and profile forms, available services, and user and group class names. For now, let's just keep it simple and define settings for the database driver, firewall name, and user class. Open the config file and append the following entries at the end of it:

```
# app/config/config.yml
fos_user:
    db_driver: orm
    firewall_name: main
    user_class: AppBundle\Entity\User
```

Adding routes

Now we need to tell Symfony where to find routes by adding the following entries to the `routing.yml` file:

```
# app/config/routing.yml
# app/config/routing.yml
fos_user:
    resource: "@FOSUserBundle/Resources/config/routing/all.xml"
```

Have a look at the contents of `all.xml`. As you can see, it contains routes for login, logout, register, password reset, edit profile, and manage groups. I will go through all of them soon.

Updating the tables

There are two main entities in `FOSUserBundle`, User and Group, and they are really rich and full of various features. To make them available to our User entity (remember that we extended ours from `FOSUserBundle`), the database schema needs to be updated. So first, drop the current tables and then create a new schema:

```
$ bin/console doctrine:schema:update --force
$ bin/console doctrine:schema:create
```

Now check the user table. As you can see in the following image, there are some extended fields in our user entity:

#	Column	Type	Collation	Attributes	Null	Default	Extra
1	**id**	int(11)			No	*None*	AUTO_INCREMENT
2	**username**	varchar(255)	utf8_unicode_ci		No	*None*	
3	**username_canonical**	varchar(255)	utf8_unicode_ci		No	*None*	
4	**email**	varchar(255)	utf8_unicode_ci		No	*None*	
5	**email_canonical**	varchar(255)	utf8_unicode_ci		No	*None*	
6	**enabled**	tinyint(1)			No	*None*	
7	**salt**	varchar(255)	utf8_unicode_ci		No	*None*	
8	**password**	varchar(255)	utf8_unicode_ci		No	*None*	
9	**last_login**	datetime			Yes	*NULL*	
10	**locked**	tinyint(1)			No	*None*	
11	**expired**	tinyint(1)			No	*None*	
12	**expires_at**	datetime			Yes	*NULL*	
13	**confirmation_token**	varchar(255)	utf8_unicode_ci		Yes	*NULL*	
14	**password_requested_at**	datetime			Yes	*NULL*	
15	**roles**	longtext	utf8_unicode_ci		No	*None*	
16	**credentials_expired**	tinyint(1)			No	*None*	
17	**credentials_expire_at**	datetime			Yes	*NULL*	

A simple road test

Visit `http://localhost:8000/login` and you will see the ugliest yet fully
functional login form ever:

layout.login
security.login.username

security.login.password

☐ security.login.remember_me | security.login.submit |

Let's deal with the labels and messages first. As you can see, the labels for input
fields here look like a yml key defined somewhere in the bundle.

That's correct and if you open the `FOSUserBundle.en.yml` file inside that bundle,
you will find the following snippet in it:

```
# mava/vendor/friendsofsymfony/UserBundle/Resources/translations/
FOSUserBundle.en.yml
# ...
security:
    login:
        username: Username
        password: Password
# ...
```

This means that whenever we hit this nested key structure, `security.login.`
`username`, the value of the key that is `Username` will be shown. Why it did not show?

This is because the translator in Symfony is deactivated by default. To activate it,
open the `config.yml` file and uncomment the following line:

```
#mava/app/config/config.yml
#...
framework:
    #esi:                ~
    translator:        { fallbacks: ["%locale%"] }
#...
```

Now if you refresh the page, you will see the values instead of keys.

As we dropped the tables in the previous topic, there is no user available to test this
bundle. Loading data fixtures won't be helpful either because there is no bio field
anymore and running the load fixtures command will give you an error.

Fortunately, `FOSUserBundle` comes with a set of commands providing all user management functionality. Run the following command to list all of them:

```
$ bin/console list fos
```

These are the available commands for the `fos` namespace:

```
fos:user:activate               Activate a user
fos:user:change-password        Change the password of a user.
fos:user:create                 Create a user.
fos:user:deactivate             Deactivate a user
fos:user:demote                 Demote a user by removing a role
fos:user:promote                Promotes a user by adding a role
```

Let's create a new user:

```
$ bin/console fos:user:create Mava info@mava.info pass --super-admin
```

I could run the command without any parameters and go through questions to set the username, e-mail, and password. Then, use the `fos:user:promote` command to set the role for the created user. However, as you can see, the preceding command does the job in one shot.

Try to log in again. It will log in but because it is redirected to the root of the website and currently no controller is defined for the home page, it throws a `404` error. I will set up login redirect later; for now, visit `/login` again and check the status bar. As you can see, it shows you as an authenticated user and if you click on the username, it shows your role as an admin:

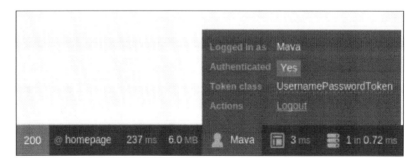

The next chapter is all about making our application look stunning. For now, let's focus on the mechanics of the project.

There is one thing that we need to take care of though. You see, after a successful login, the user will be redirected to the root of the website that is the default welcome page. What would be more appropriate is redirecting to a dashboard page. Let's see how we can fix this. Before this, we need to address broken data fixtures.

Generating automated data fixtures

So far, we had only four entities and only one of them changed in structure. However, we spent some effort creating data fixtures for them.

Besides, defining the relationship in each data fixture is a delicate job. Imagine how complex it becomes as the number of entities and their relationship grows in a project. There should be a better way to create data fixtures.

Introducing AliceBundle

AliceBundle wraps around the Alice library that is created to handle data fixtures. With AliceBundle, we can create and modify data fixtures and their relationship in a clean and dynamic way. In other words, we don't need to create bulky PHP classes for data fixtures. A simple yml file will do a way better job with Alice. The good news is that doctrine/data fixture commands are still useful, so we can use the same load command without changing anything.

1. Start by installing and configuring AliceBundle:

   ```
   $ composer require --dev hautelook/alice-bundle doctrine/data-
   fixtures
   ```

2. Add it to AppKernel.php:

   ```php
   // mava/app/AppKernel.php
   <?php
   public function registerBundles()
   {
       //...
       if (in_array($this->getEnvironment(), ['dev', 'test'])) {
           //...
           $bundles[] =
               new Hautelook\AliceBundle\HautelookAliceBundle();
       }
       //...
   }
   ```

You may notice the dev option in the installation command that we used. This is because we need the data fixtures only in dev and test environments. This is why we activate it only in these environments in AppKernel.php.

Now, add the following configurations for Alice (notice that we are using config_dev.yml):

```
# app/config/config_dev.yml
hautelook_alice:
    db_drivers:
        orm: ~        # Enable Doctrine ORM if is registered
    locale: en_US  # Locale to used for faker
    seed: 1     # A seed to make sure faker generates data consistently
    persist_once: false # Only persist objects once
    loading_limit: 5    # Max times the loader try to load the files
```

Creating data fixtures with Alice

Before defining new fixtures, go to the AppBundle/DataFixture/ORM subfolder and remove all the previous data fixtures. Now, you can start afresh and add a new data fixture for the user entity with the following contents:

```
# src/AppBundle/DataFixtures/ORM/app.yml
AppBundle\Entity\User:
    user{1..10}:
        username: <userName()>
        email: <email()>
        password: <password()>
```

Compare these few lines with the long php class that we used to have for datafixtures and you will appreciate the power of Alice. Now load this fixture as follows:

```
$ bin/console hautelook_alice:doctrine:fixtures:load
```

You can call a shorter version as follows:

```
$ bin/console h:d:f:l
```

Check your user table in the database and you will see that there are 10 new records with random contents sitting here:

The contents of the data-fixture file should be self-explanatory. User{1..10} creates a loop for user generation and repeats it 10 times. Of course, you can change the number to whatever you like. For the user entity that extends FOSUserBundle, we have three mandatory fields: username, e-mail, and password. As you can see, there is a fake content generator for each field and luckily it uses the same field name. For example, username: <userName()> means that we want to generate a random username with the userName() function.

Where do these functions come from? Behind the scenes, AliceBundle uses a library called **Faker** that generates all of these fake fields. To see a complete list of available fields, check the following link:

https://github.com/fzaninotto/Faker

Relationship with Alice

Creating dynamic data fixtures with Alice is really helpful but not good enough. For example, Workspace to Project has a one-to-many relationship. How can we define this relationship in the generated data fixtures?

Defining relationships in Alice is as simple as adding an @ symbol in front of the field name. Open the previous app.yml data-fixtures file and modify it as follows:

```
# src/AppBundle/DataFixtures/ORM/app.yml
AppBundle\Entity\User:
    user{1..10}:
        username: <userName()>
        email: <email()>
        password: <password()>
AppBundle\Entity\Workspace:
```

```
    workspace{1..3}:
        name: <word()>
        description: <text()>
AppBundle\Entity\Project:
    project{1..7}:
        title: <word()>
        description: <text()>
        dueDate: <dateTimeBetween($startDate = 'now', $endDate = '+9
days')>
        workspace: "@workspace*"
AppBundle\Entity\Task:
    task{1..15}:
        title: <word()>
        description: <text()>
        dueDate: <dateTimeBetween($startDate = 'now', $endDate = '+3
months')>
        attachment: <boolean($chanceOfGettingTrue = 50)>
        project: "@project*"
        user: "@user*"
```

Load the new data-fixture:

```
$ bin/console h:d:f:l
Careful, database will be purged. Do you want to continue y/N ?y
  > fixtures found:
      - /var/www/packt/mava/src/AppBundle/DataFixtures/ORM/app.yml
  > purging database
  > fixtures loaded
```

Now check the tables and you will find that tons of records are generated and they have a relationship with records from other tables as well.

What would be ideal is to replace contents of the test database and update the `dump.sql` file in the `tests/_data` folder. This way, the test environment will benefit from our new data fixtures as well. To see how to do this, refer to the previous chapter.

Setting up the login redirection

With the new data fixtures in place, let's go back to the login functionality and deal with its required features. What a user normally wants to see after login is his personal dashboard area. So let's make a simple Dashboard controller for it. Before writing any code, we need to act like a professional and create the tests first.

Creating tests for the new controller

What we need here is a new controller for the dashboard with a simple `indexAction` method that simply renders a basic template containing a placeholder message.

So create an outline for a unit test:

```
$ vendor/bin/codecept g:test unit DashboardController
Test was created in mava/tests/unit/DashboardControllerTest.php
```

Edit the file as follows:

```php
// mava/tests/unit/ DashboardControllerTest.php
<?php
class DashboardControllerTest extends \Codeception\TestCase\Test
{
    /**
     * @var \UnitTester
     */
    protected $tester;
    public function testShowAction()
    {
        $this->tester->amOnRoute('dashboard_index');
        $this->tester->seeResponseContains(
          'This is a placeholder for dashboard area.');
    }
}
```

Now create the functional test:

```
$ vendor/bin/codecept generate:cest functional DashboardController
Test was created in mava/tests/functional/DashboardControllerCest.php
```

Add the following contents to it:

```php
// mava/tests/functional/DashboardControllerCest.php
<?php
class DashboardControllerCest
{
    public function testShowAction(FunctionalTester $I)
    {
        $I->wantTo('too see inside the dashboard area');
        $I->amOnPage('/dashboard');
        $I->see('a placeholder for dashboard');
    }
}
```

Finally, create the acceptance test:

```
$ vendor/bin/codecept g:cest acceptance DashboardController
Test was created in mava/tests/acceptance/DashboardControllerCest.php
```

Edit it as follows:

```
mava/tests/acceptance/DashboardControllerCest.php
<?php
class DashboardControllerCest
{
    public function testShowAction(AcceptanceTester $I)
    {
        $I->wantTo('too see inside the dashboard area');
        $I->amOnPage('/dashboard');
        $I->see('a placeholder for dashboard');
        $I->wait(3);
    }
}
```

The functional and acceptance tests are almost identical. The only difference between them is that the acceptance test runs in a browser. The unit test looks similar to the other two as well, except that it checks the response contents and not the template. It will be a stepping stone to create more robust tests later when we add more functionality to it.

If we run the tests, they will fail. This is great because now we have a direction to go in.

 Note that we altered the user table. This means that the data fixtures that we created before are not valid anymore and the SQL code to create schema in the test environment should be updated again. Refer to the previous chapter to see how to create a new `dump.sql` file.

Creating the Dashboard Controller

Add a new controller and edit its contents as follows:

```
// mava/src/AppBundle/Controller/DashboardController.php
<?php
namespace AppBundle\Controller;
use Sensio\Bundle\FrameworkExtraBundle\Configuration\Route;
use Symfony\Bundle\FrameworkBundle\Controller\Controller;
use Symfony\Component\HttpFoundation\Response;
```

```
class DashboardController extends Controller
{
    /**
     * @Route("/dashboard", name="dashboard_index")
     * @return Response
     */
    public function indexAction()
    {
        return $this->render('dashboard/index.html.twig');
    }
}
```

The `twig` file that it needs to render could be a placeholder as follows:

```
{# mava/app/Resources/views/dashboard/index.html.twig #}
<p>This is a placeholder for dashboard area.</p>
```

Finally, we need to tell the security system that we are willing to be redirected to the dashboard after login:

```
# app/config/security.yml
security:
# ...
    firewalls:
        # ...
        main:
            form_login:
                # ...
                # change the default page to monitor page
                default_target_path: dashboard_index
```

Now execute the selenium first:

```
$ java -jar path/to/selenium-server-standalone.jar
```

Then, run all three tests again:

```
$ vendor/bin/codecept run unit DashboardControllerTest
```

```
$ vendor/bin/codecept run functional DashboardControllerCest
```

```
$ vendor/bin/codecept run acceptance DashboardControllerCest
```

They all pass, but we have two problems here. First, the dashboard route is not firewalled so everyone can see it without logging in to the system. Besides, the entities that we have created so far should be organized inside the dashboard. This means that the route to access a workspace should be something like /dashboard/workspace/{id}.

Securing the dashboard

We can update the current controller's routes and add a /dashboard prefix to them to fix the organizing problem. After updating the routes, all we need to do is secure the dashboard itself. As a result, the routes in other controllers will be firewalled as well.

Fix the access control for the dashboard first. Open security.yml and add a single line at the end of it:

```
# app/config/security.yml
security:
    # ...
    access_control:
        # ...
        - { path: ^/dashboard/, role: IS_AUTHENTICATED_FULLY }
```

This means that only logged in users can access the dashboard and beyond. Now modify annotation routes in WorkspaceController as follows:

```php
<?php
// ...
/**
 * @Route("/dashboard/workspace")
 */
class WorkspaceController extends Controller
{
    /**
     * @Route("/{name}", name="workspace_show")
     */
    public function showAction($name)
    {
        //....
    }
}
```

By adding a global route for the class itself, this route will be applied to every method inside it. This way, we secure any controller that hits the /dashboard/* pattern.

The Sonata project

The frontend security is partially in place. So let's see how we can manage the user and other contents from the admin area. To do so, we need an admin dashboard with CRUD functionality, not only for users, but also for other entities created so far.

According to packagist.org, after `FOSUserBundle`, the most popular Symfony bundle is `SonataAdminBundle`. You can find more about the Sonata project at `https://sonata-project.org`.

The Sonata project was originally founded by Thomas Rabiax and its main aim was creating an e-commerce solution. Today, it consists of a couple of bundles that help create blogs, handle media files, backend administration, and much more. In this chapter, we will look at `SonataAdminBundle` and then use `SonataUserBundle` to integrate `FOSUserBundle` into the admin area.

Installing and configuring Sonata bundle

As usual, install the bundle and its dependencies and activate them all in the kernel:

```
$ composer require sonata-project/admin-bundle "dev-master"
```

When you run this command, there are other bundles such as `SonataCoreBundle`, `KnpMenuBundle`, `BlockBundle`, and others that will be downloaded and installed automatically.

As we are using doctrine, we need to install the following bundle for database interaction:

```
$ composer require sonata-project/doctrine-orm-admin-bundle
```

We need to install `dev-master` branch.

> If you are wondering why we used `dev-master` here, that's because, at the time of writing this chapter, there are many works in progress in the Sonata project to make it compatible with Symfony 3. At this time, only the `dev-master` branch works with Symfony 3.0.

Now, open the `AppKernel.php` file and add the new bundles as follows:

```php
// app/AppKernel.php
public function registerBundles()
{
  return array(
    // ...
    new Sonata\CoreBundle\SonataCoreBundle(),
    new Sonata\BlockBundle\SonataBlockBundle(),

    new Knp\Bundle\MenuBundle\KnpMenuBundle(),
    new Sonata\DoctrineORMAdminBundle\SonataDoctrineORMAdminBundle(),
    new Sonata\AdminBundle\SonataAdminBundle(),
  );
}
```

In Sonata, almost everything is represented as a block. All required blocks should be defined under the `sonata_block` key in the `config.yml` file:

```
# app/config/config.yml
sonata_block:
    default_contexts: [cms]
    blocks:
        # Enable the SonataAdminBundle block
        sonata.admin.block.admin_list:
            contexts:     [admin]
```

Now install all the new assets and then clear the cache:

```
$ bin/console assets:install web
$ bin/console cache:clear
```

We will deal with security later; for now, let's add the routes and check the admin URL. Open the `routing.yml` file and add the following contents to it:

```
# app/config/routing.yml
# ...
admin_area:
    resource: '@SonataAdminBundle/Resources/config/routing/sonata_
admin.xml'
    prefix: /admin
```

Let's see if it works by visiting `http://localhost:8000/admin`:

It works! I agree that it is very quiet at the moment and nothing is there, but it is a real admin dashboard. In the next topic, I will show you how to flesh it out and make it do something.

Adding contents to the dashboard

In the simplest form, creating manageable contents in the dashboard is a three-step process. I will do that for workspace and project entities and you can follow the same process for the rest of the entities that we have so far. (The same process applies to the entities that will be introduced in the following chapters.)

You can check the completed code for this chapter on the GitHub repository. Each chapter is tagged with 0.1.[chapter number] format. For example, the tag for Chapter 6 is 0.1.6.

1. All admin contents for each bundle are kept inside the `Admin` folder, so create this folder and add a new class for workspaces as follows:

```php
<?php
//  src/AppBundle/Admin/WorkspaceAdmin.php
namespace AppBundle\Admin;

use Sonata\AdminBundle\Admin\Admin;
use Sonata\AdminBundle\Datagrid\ListMapper;
use Sonata\AdminBundle\Datagrid\DatagridMapper;
use Sonata\AdminBundle\Form\FormMapper;

class WorkspaceAdmin extends Admin
{
  // Fields to be shown on create/edit forms
  protected function configureFormFields(FormMapper $formMapper)
    {
        $formMapper
            ->add('name', 'text')
            ->add('description','textarea');
    }

  // Fields to be shown on filter forms
  protected function configureDatagridFilters(
                      DatagridMapper $datagridMapper)
    {
        $datagridMapper
            ->add('name')
            ->add('description');
    }

  // Fields to be shown on lists
  protected function configureListFields(
                      ListMapper $listMapper)
    {
        $listMapper
            ->addIdentifier('name')
            ->add('description');
    }
}
```

I will cover the forms in *Chapter 8, Deployment process Project Review*. Here, you can see how Sonata benefits from it by mapping entity properties to a form or list.

2. An important thing about the admin area is that it should be called a service. Like I mentioned before, I have a whole chapter about services and dependency injection. For now, just create this service by adding a new file to your application's `config` folder:

```
# app/config/services.yml
#...
services:
    admin.workspace:
        class: AppBundle\Admin\WorkspaceAdmin
        arguments: [~, AppBundle\Entity\Workspace, ~]
        tags:
            - { name: sonata.admin, manager_type: orm, label:
Workspace }
```

3. SonataAdminBundle generates routes for each entity that we add to the admin area. So we only need to add one general route for all the entities as follows:

```
# mava/app/config/routing.yml
_sonata_admin:
    resource: .
    type: sonata_admin
    prefix: /admin
#...
```

4. That's it! Visit the admin area again and you will see the workspace entity there and you can CRUD it:

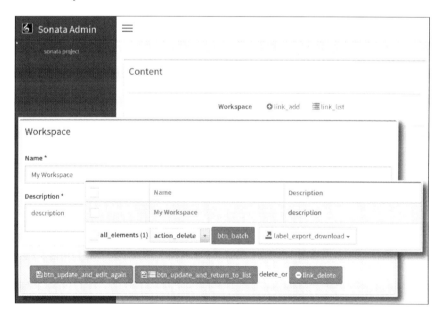

Creating admin feature for entities with relations

The workspace entity was easy because it didn't have any dependency on other entities. What about entities such as project that has a column, `workspace_id`, that defines its many-to-one relations with workspace?

For these kinds of entities, you just need to modify the form mapper; the rest of the admin definition process is the same:

```php
<?php
//  mava/src/AppBundle/Admin/ProjectAdmin.php
// ...

class ProjectAdmin extends Admin
{
  // Fields to be shown on create/edit forms
  protected function configureFormFields(FormMapper $formMapper)
    {
        $formMapper
            ->add('title' , 'text')
            ->add('description', 'textarea')
            ->add('workspace','entity',
                array(
                    'class' => 'AppBundle\Entity\Workspace',
                    'property' => 'name'
                ))
            ->add('dueDate', 'date',
                array(
                    'input'  => 'datetime',
                    'widget' => 'single_text',
                    'format' => 'yyyy-MM-dd',
                ));
    }
  // ...
}
```

Pay attention to the `workspace` field. It is defined as an entity and points to the `workspace` entity class. However, mentioning the class is not enough because HTML forms cannot understand entities and show the whole entity in a form field. So by setting `property` to `name`, we tell the form builder that we don't need the whole entity, just show `workspace.name`.

Integrating FOSUserBundle into the admin area

So far, we created a login system using FOSUserBundle and an entity manager area via SonataAdminBundle. So, the application has an admin area that has its access limits set to ROLE_ADMIN people only. Before creating a dashboard for users so that they can manage their workspaces, projects, tasks, and team members, there is one last important thing that needs to be done. An admin should be able to manage all users from the backend.

The Sonata project comes with a bundle that integrates FOSUserBundle into the admin area. It is called SonataUserBundle that basically adds some features to FOSUserBundle and makes it part of the backend.

Installing SonataUserBundle

Start by downloading and installing it:

```
$ composer require sonata-project/user-bundle 'dev-master'
```

> The installation might fail because of datagrid-bundle. If you are prompted for this issue, install datagrid-bundle first then continue with user-bundle:
>
> composer require sonata-project/datagrid-bundle 'dev-master'

Activating this bundle in AppKernel.php is a little different from what we have done so far. As we are going to extend FOSUserBundle, the code should look as follows:

```php
<?php
// app/AppKernel.php
public function registerbundles()
{
    return array(
        // ...
        new Sonata\UserBundle\SonataUserBundle('FOSUserBundle'),
        // ...
    );
}
```

Yes, it should have FOSUserBundle as its parameter.

SonataUserBundle configuration

One of the `SonataUserBundle` features is providing user groups and ACLs. **Access Control List (ACL)** and this is where you define which group of users can have access to what types of resources and what kind of access (CRUD) they can have.

In the following lines, the basic configuration setup for user groups is provided:

```
# app/config/config.yml
fos_user:
    #...
    user_class:       AppBundle\Entity\User

    group:
        group_class:    AppBundle\Entity\Group
        group_manager: sonata.user.orm.group_manager

    service:
        user_manager: sonata.user.orm.user_manager
```

As you can see, they are defined under the `fos_user` key. Remember that `SonataUserBundle` is a wrapper for `FOSUserBundle`. That's why all definitions should go here.

It is not all about FOS. In the same configuration file, we need to add some Sonata settings as well. First, add some blocks to add the menu and login options to user profiles in the dashboard:

```
# app/config/config.yml
sonata_block:
  blocks:
      # ...
      sonata.user.block.menu:    # shows menu in profile page
      sonata.user.block.account: # shows login option in the menu
```

The last configuration is to activate ACLs:

```
#app/config/config.yml
sonata_user:
    security_acl: true
    manager_type: orm
```

ACL is related to security, so add the `acl` key to `app/config/security.yml` as follows:

```
# app/config/security.yml
security:
```

```
# ...
acl:
    connection: default
```

One of the most important parts of configuration is letting doctrine know about the entity mappings for your bundle and `SonataUserBundle`:

```
#app/config/config.yml
doctrine:
  dbal:
    types:
      json: Sonata\Doctrine\Types\JsonType

  orm:
    entity_managers:
      default:
        auto_mapping: true
```

Updating the routes

By installing `SonataUserBundle`, we don't need FOS routes anymore because Sonata will take over from here. So, to prevent any conflicts, replace the following lines.

The file to be edited: `app/config/routing.yml`

- fos_user_security:

  ```
  resource: "@FOSUserBundle/Resources/config/routing/security.
  xml"
  ```

- fos_user_profile:

  ```
  resource: "@FOSUserBundle/Resources/config/routing/profile.
  xml"
  prefix: /profile
  ```

- fos_user_register:

  ```
  resource: "@FOSUserBundle/Resources/config/routing/
  registration.xml"
  prefix: /register
  ```

- fos_user_resetting:

  ```
  resource: "@FOSUserBundle/Resources/config/routing/resetting.
  xml"
  prefix: /resetting
  ```

- fos_user_change_password:

  ```
      resource: "@FOSUserBundle/Resources/config/routing/change_
  password.xml"
      prefix: /profile
  ```

Replace the preceding lines with these routes.

The file to be edited: `app/config/routing.yml`

- sonata_user_security:

  ```
      resource: "@SonataUserBundle/Resources/config/routing/sonata_
  security_1.xml"
  ```

- sonata_user_resetting:

  ```
      resource: "@SonataUserBundle/Resources/config/routing/ sonata_
  resetting_1.xml"
      prefix: /resetting
  ```

- sonata_user_profile:

  ```
      resource: "@SonataUserBundle/Resources/config/routing/sonata_
  profile_1.xml"
      prefix: /profile
  ```

- sonata_user_register:

  ```
      resource: "@SonataUserBundle/Resources/config/routing/sonata_
  registration_1.xml"
      prefix: /register
  ```

- sonata_user_change_password:

  ```
      resource: "@SonataUserBundle/Resources/config/routing/sonata_
  change_password_1.xml"
      prefix: /profile
  ```

It is important to integrate `SonataUserBundle` into the admin area. Create another route to do this:

sonata_user:

```
    resource: '@SonataUserBundle/Resources/config/routing/admin_
security.xml'
    prefix: /admin
```

Setting the security

Now we have two ways to log in:

- Log in to the frontend that our customers will use to access their accounts, define workspaces, projects, and so on

- Log in to the backend that only admins can access

This means that a firewall for the backend is necessary. Besides, with `SonataUserBundle` on board, the role hierarchy should change accordingly.

Open `app/config/security.yml` and modify roles as follows:

```
# app/config/security.yml
security:
    #...
    role_hierarchy:
        ROLE_ADMIN:          [ROLE_USER, ROLE_SONATA_ADMIN]
        ROLE_SUPER_ADMIN:  [ROLE_ADMIN, ROLE_ALLOWED_TO_SWITCH]
```

Under `firewalls`, create a new key and call it `admin`. This is where login/logout settings for the admin area are defined:

```
# app/config/security.yml
    firewalls:
    #...
        admin:
            pattern:            ^/admin/
            context:            user
            form_login:
                provider:       fos_userbundle
                login_path:     /admin/login
                use_forward:    false
                check_path:     /admin/login_check
                failure_path:   null
            logout:
                path:           /admin/logout
            anonymous:          true
```

The last task here is setting the access control for the backend. Find the `access_control` key and replace its contents as follows:

```
# app/config/security.yml
security:
    access_control:
```

```
        # URL of FOSUserBundle which need to be available to anonymous
users
        - { path: ^/login$, role: IS_AUTHENTICATED_ANONYMOUSLY }
        - { path: ^/register, role: IS_AUTHENTICATED_ANONYMOUSLY }
        - { path: ^/resetting, role: IS_AUTHENTICATED_ANONYMOUSLY }

        # Admin login page needs to be access without credential
        - { path: ^/admin/login$, role: IS_AUTHENTICATED_ANONYMOUSLY }
        - { path: ^/admin/logout$, role: IS_AUTHENTICATED_ANONYMOUSLY
}
        - { path: ^/admin/login_check$, role: IS_AUTHENTICATED_
ANONYMOUSLY }

        # Secured part of the site
        # This config requires being logged for the whole site and
having the admin role for the admin part.
        # Change these rules to adapt them to your needs
        - { path: ^/admin/, role: [ROLE_ADMIN, ROLE_SONATA_ADMIN] }
        - { path: ^/.*, role: IS_AUTHENTICATED_ANONYMOUSLY }
```

Checking the installation

Try to access the admin area by visiting `http://localhost:8000/admin/ dashboard`. This time, it will show a totally different login form.

Fill in the form with credentials and, if your user has an admin role, you will see the following screen:

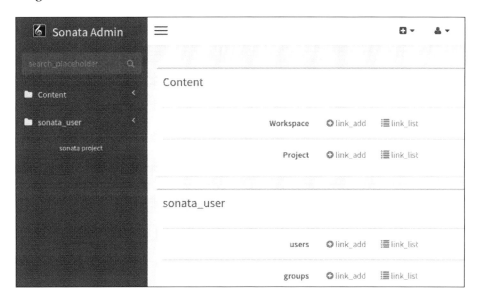

Putting SonataUserBundle in charge

We have two bundles at the moment that can manage users. What we need to do is transfer user management from FOS to Sonata.

1. First of all, the User entity needs to be updated. This means that it should not extend from the FOS User entity anymore. Instead, it should extend from the Sonata User entity:

```php
<?php
// mava/src/AppBundle/Entity/User.php

namespace AppBundle\Entity;

use Doctrine\ORM\Mapping as ORM;
use Sonata\UserBundle\Entity\BaseUser

/**
 * User
 * @ORM\Table(name="mava_user")
 * @ORM\Entity(repositoryClass="AppBundle\Entity\UserRepository")
 */
class User extends BaseUser
{
    /**
     * @var integer
     * @ORM\Column(name="id", type="integer")
     * @ORM\Id
     * @ORM\GeneratedValue(strategy="AUTO")
     */
    protected $id;

    public function __construct()
    {
        parent::__construct();
    }

}
```

2. Groups are already defined in `app/config.yml` so we need to create an entity for them:

```php
<?php
// mava/src/AppBundle/Entity/Group.php
namespace AppBundle\Entity;
use Doctrine\ORM\Mapping as ORM;
use Sonata\UserBundle\Entity\BaseGroup;

/**
 * Group
 * @ORM\Table(name="group")
 * @ORM\Entity
 */
class Group extends BaseGroup
{
    /**
     * @var integer
     * @ORM\Column(type="integer")
     * @ORM\Id
     * @ORM\GeneratedValue(strategy="AUTO")
     */
    protected $id;

    /**
     * Get id
     * @return  integer
     */
    public function getId()
    {
        return $this->id;
    }
}
```

3. Before continuing, let's update the tables and see what the User table looks when it is extended from SonataUserBundle:

```
$ bin/console doctrine:schema:update –force
```

Check the `user` table now and you will see that a huge amount of columns, 39 columns to be specific, have been added to it:

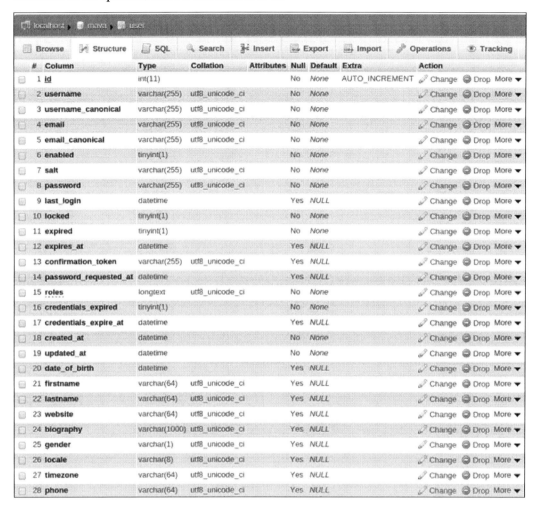

We just need some of them, so in the next topic, we will see how to configure the admin area for the User entity.

There is a lot to say about User and Group management. However, let's finish the basic functionality of the task management itself. In *Chapter 8*, *Project Review* we will come back to User management again and see how to define ACLs and benefit from it in User and Groups. Moreover, it is critical to be able to edit user profiles, set up registration and forgotten password functionality, and send confirmation e-mails from the website. These topics will be covered too.

User dashboard

A good web application for task management is not complete with an admin area for only the backend. Every individual member needs his own dashboard too. This means that a member should be able to manage his own projects and tasks in his own workspaces without having access to the backend.

Let's say that all frontend activities should be kept inside the /dashboard URL. The good news is that we already set up the firewall for the dashboard. As you remember, these settings are done in security.yml:

```
firewalls:
    # ...
    main:
        pattern:            .*
        context:            user
        form_login:
            provider:       fos_userbundle
            login_path:     /login
            use_forward:    false
            check_path:     /login_check
            failure_path:   null
        logout:             true
        anonymous:          true
access_control:
    # ...
    # Secured part of the site
    - { path: ^/, role: IS_AUTHENTICATED_FULLY }
```

All we need to do is create **Controllers** and related actions to deal with workspace, project, task, and member requests.

Generating CRUD

Without getting into much trouble, generate CRUD for all four entities so far. This will be the basic structure of what we need. We will build the rest of our controllers on top of it. I will show you the settings for Workspace and you can do the same for the rest of entities (or get the finished codes from the 0.1.6 tag in the GitHub repository):

```
$ bin/console doctrine:generate:crud

The Entity shortcut name: AppBundle:Workspace

Do you want to generate the "write" actions [no]? yes

Configuration format (yml,xml,php or annotation) [annotation]: yml
```

```
Routes prefix [/workspace]:
Confirm automatic update of the Routing [yes]?
Importing the CRUD routes: OK
```

As you can see, I chose yml for the configuration file to keep everything consistent.

This command added a new resource to the bundle's `routing.yml` file:

```
# src/Mava/CoreBundle/Resources/config/routing.yml
#...
core_workspace:
    resource: "@AppBundle/Resources/config/routing/workspace.yml"
    prefix:   /workspace
#...
```

This resource contains all the required routes to list, create, update, and delete workspaces:

```
# mava/src/AppBundle/Resources/config/routing/workspace.yml
```

- workspace:
  ```
  path:     /
  defaults: { _controller: "AppBundle:Workspace:index" }
  ```

- workspace_show:
  ```
  path:     /{id}/show
  defaults: { _controller: "AppBundle:Workspace:show" }
  ```

- workspace_new:
  ```
  path:     /new
  defaults: { _controller: "AppBundle:Workspace:new" }
  ```

- workspace_create:
  ```
  path:     /create
  defaults: { _controller: "AppBundle:Workspace:create" }
  requirements: { _method: post }
  ```

- workspace_edit:
  ```
  path:     /{id}/edit
  defaults: { _controller: "AppBundle:Workspace:edit" }
  ```

- workspace_update:
  ```
  path:     /{id}/update
  defaults: { _controller: "AppBundle:Workspace:update" }
  requirements: { _method: post|put }
  ```

- workspace_delete:

```
path:      /{id}/delete
defaults: { _controller: "AppBundle:Workspace:delete" }
requirements: { _method: post|delete }
```

> It is good to organize entity-related routes in separate
> resources and import them as they are required. Imagine
> how messy the bundle's main `routing.yml` file will look if
> we save all the routes here.

Apart from new routes, there is a new controller, form, and a couple of templates generated by the previous command. By default, the controller will be in charge of database commands and the form will show the required forms to show, create, and edit each entity. How they will be shown is decided in the templates for each entity.

> This is not ideal. As you may remember, a good controller is a lean
> one. So putting business logic in a controller is very bad practice.
> They are supposed to be kept inside repository files (that is,
> `WorkspaceRepository.php`) or ideally, they should be defined
> as a service, which I will show you how to do in *Chapter 9, Services
> and Service Containers*. For now, just accept the default settings. We
> will have a lot to do in the coming chapters.

Modifying the forms

Assuming that you have generated CRUDs for all the available entities, you may notice that some of them don't work the way you expected. For example, if you visit `/project/new`, an exception will be thrown:

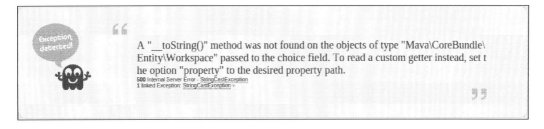

In case you generated CRUD for the User entity as well, only the `id` property will be shown if you visit any of the `/user` routes, and none of those impressive columns in as shown in the image of the *Checking the installation* section are available here.

Fixing the project form is easy. Actually, we did that at the beginning of this chapter already. The problem is that an HTML form does not understand and cannot accept the who entity as a value for an element. So we need to choose one property from an entity and pass it to the form element. Open the ProjectType.php file and modify the Workspace field as follows:

```php
<?php
// mava/src/AppBunlde/Form/ProjectType.php
class ProjectType extends AbstractType
{
    public function buildForm(FormBuilderInterface $builder,
                                array $options)
    {
        $builder
            //...
            ->add('workspace','entity',
                array(
                    'class' => 'AppBundle/Entity/Workspace',
                    'property' => 'name'
                ));
    }
//...
```

Do we need to fix User forms? The more important question is did you need to generate CRUD for it? As you know, the User entity was extended from SonataUserBundle. This means that it has its own controllers, forms, and templates to edit the user profile, change the password, and and so on.

So, technically, we didn't have to generate CRUD for this entity in the first place. However, if, for any reason, you needed to generate CRUD for it, then you have to create the required forms, controllers, and templates yourself.

Summary

In this chapter, we saw the very basics of security in Symfony. You learned that security is a two-step process where authentication verifies that a user is genuine and authorization decides that parts of a website can be accessed by an authenticated user.

We used FOSUserBundle to implement a frontend user management system. Then, we installed SonataAdminBundle and its dependencies to create a backend dashboard and admin services for our entities. Finally, we integrated FOSUserBundle into the backend through SonataUserBundle.

The next chapter is all about making the project look pretty. With a functional template, we can tackle some functional tests as well and see the continuous integration progress while carrying on with development.

7
The Presentation Layer

This chapter explains how templates are created, extended, included, and displayed in Symfony. We will start with base templates and then add layers and layers of other components on top of it. The other important subject that we will discuss in this chapter is the popular frontend framework called Bootstrap. The Bootstrap framework is a slick and modern frontend package, which almost every new web application benefits from. We will see how to integrate and use this framework in Symfony.

We will also see how to use Symfony's amazing asset management component, `Assetic`, to organize images, .css, and .js files and, at the same time, optimize the project performance.

After the basic appearance of the project has been created in this chapter, we will be ready to modify or add new functionality to each page in the following chapters.

How assets are organized

When you look at bundles in Symfony, you might think this is one big mess. How can you possibly get things working while there are so many `Resources/` folders all over the place and each of them contains a set of templates, .css, and .js files?

Here is the situation: there are some assets that belong to the bundles created by us. There are other assets that came with a vendor when we installed a third-party bundle, and finally there are some assets that belong to the project globally and cannot be saved in any specific bundle. The question is how to organize them.

Have a look in the `web/` directory and you will find the answer. As you can see, all resources that have been used so far in this project are sitting there. So, technically, Symfony does not need to look in each bundle individually to find an image, for example. Actually, this is the best way to do it. If you decide to use a bundle somewhere else, you just install it there and you don't need to look for its resources in your project. After installation, you simply copy its assets to the `web/` folder via `assets:install` (or create a symbolic link to them: `assets:install -symlink`). However, in this project, I am going to follow best practices offered by official Symfony documents. For each bundle that I create myself, I am going to move all its assets (templates, css, and js files) to the `app/Resources` directory. Then, I will use `Assetic` to manage everything for me.

Asset management

Getting a better performance from a framework is not all about the backend. The frontend is as important, if not more. It is critical to optimize images, reduce file I/O, and cache the contents to speed up the loading time.

As you know, there are many frontend tools such as LESS that help optimize the frontend performance. How do we do it in Symfony? `AsseticBundle` is designed to manage assets and optimize the speed for us. It uses various techniques to do this. For example, a large JavaScript file might have hundreds of lines of mutable code that we don't need to load for a specific task. So, we can filter out unwanted code and reduce the load time. The other scenario could be a group of JavaScript functions that are saved in various .js files. If we could combine all of them into one file and filter only what we need, then we can improve the performance radically. Well, that's what Assetic does.

In the older versions of Symfony, this bundle was shipped with it by default, but from Symfony 2.8 onward, we need to install it.

 Note that in case the Assetic bundle is deprecated in the future or if you prefer to use your favorite asset manager such as Bower instead of Assetic, you can follow this guide and integrate the asset manager of your choice with your Symfony project:

http://symfony.com/doc/current/cookbook/frontend/bower.html

As usual, use the composer to install and register it in `AppKernel.php`:

```
$ composer require symfony/assetic-bundle

// app/AppKernel.php
// ...
```

```
class AppKernel extends Kernel
{
    // ...
    public function registerBundles()
    {
        $bundles = array(
            // ...
            new Symfony\Bundle\AsseticBundle\AsseticBundle(),
        );
        // ...
    }
}
```

Now configure it as follows:

```
# app/config/config.yml
assetic:
    debug:           '%kernel.debug%'
    use_controller:  '%kernel.debug%'
    filters:
        cssrewrite: ~
        less:
            node: /usr/bin/node
            node_paths: [/usr/lib/node_modules]
            apply_to: "\.less$"
# ...
```

As you can see, we activated two filters at the moment. We will see how to use `assetic` filters and apply them to a group of resources as we continue.

How templates are organized

The strategy that you choose for template hierarchy depends on your project. In this project, we will place the base template on the base of the pyramid. This is where you define the main HTML structure of your project. It contains the building blocks of your main template. This means placeholders for blocks such as headers, navigation, body, and footer are defined here.

So, we cannot define an important template like this in our bundles. It should be somewhere safe where it can be easily accessible from every corner of the project.

The `app/Resources/views` folder seems to be the perfect place for it. Define your desired skeleton for projects here, then extend it in your bundles and add content the way you like. This way, if you need to modify the page structure in the future, you don't need to go through every single bundle individually. As they are extended from the base template, changing the base will affect the rest of the templates.

How about vendors? You can easily extend the base template in your own bundle and do whatever you like with them. However, to modify anything in the `vendors/` directory is evil. As an example, imagine that you need to modify the profile edit template that is available in `SonataUserBundle` and make some changes. How would you do this without touching it in the `vendors/` directory? The answer is in the `app/Resources` folder again. Just create a new folder and name it after your desired bundle. Any change that you make here will be used by Symfony to override the original template. In this chapter, I will show you how to override templates in third party bundles.

Let's mold the clay

A good base template shouldn't have anything other than blocks. This means that if you have a class name or ID name defined in your base template, then you need to reconsider your structure. Yes, your code still works but it does not follow the best practices. Remember, a base template is supposed to define the structure only. So, all styling or functional-related contents should be kept in the children templates that extend the base.

Keeping this in mind, let's modify the default base template a little:

```
{# app/Resources/views/base.html.twig #}
<!DOCTYPE html>
<html>
    <head>
        <meta charset="UTF-8"/>
        <title>{% block title %}{% endblock %}</title>
        {% block head %}{% endblock %}
    </head>
    <body>
        {% block navigation %}{% endblock %}
        {% block body %}{% endblock %}
        {% block footer %}{% endblock %}
        {% block javascripts %}{% endblock %}
    </body>
</html>
```

It does not have any reference to assets, so let's add another template for them. Name this file `mavaBase.html.twig` and save it in the same place where the base template lives:

```
{# app/Resources/views/mava_base.html.twig #}
{% extends "base.html.twig" %}
{% block title 'MAVA' %}
```

```twig
{% block head %}
    <link rel="icon" sizes="16x16" href="{{ asset('favicon.ico') }}"
/>
    {% if app.environment == 'prod' %}
        {# Compile all CSS into 1 file #}
        {% stylesheets
                '@bootstrap_css'
                '@mava_css'
                output='css/compiled/main.css' %}
            <link rel="stylesheet" href="{{ asset_url }}" />
        {% endstylesheets %}
    {% else %}
        {# Ask Assetic to generate the files individually #}
        {% stylesheets '@bootstrap_css'
            output='css/bootstrap.css' %}
            <link rel="stylesheet" href="{{ asset_url }}" />
        {% endstylesheets %}
        {% stylesheets '@mava_css' output='css/mava.css' %}
            <link rel="stylesheet" href="{{ asset_url }}" />
        {% endstylesheets %}
    {% endif %}
{% endblock %}
{% block javascripts %}
    {% if app.environment == 'prod' %}
        {# Compile all JS into 1 file #}
        {% javascripts
                '@jquery'
                '@bootstrap_js'
                output='js/compiled/main.js' %}
            <script src="{{ asset_url }}"></script>
        {% endjavascripts %}
    {% else %}
        {# Ask Assetic to generate the files  individually #}
        {% javascripts '@jquery' output='js/jquery.js' %}
        {% endjavascripts %}
        {% javascripts '@bootstrap_js' output='js/bootstrap.js' %}
        {% endjavascripts %}
        {# Reference the generated files #}
        <script src="{{ asset('js/jquery.js') }}"></script>
        <script src="{{ asset('js/bootstrap.js') }}"></script>
    {% endif %}
{% endblock %}
```

Imagine how big and ugly the `base.html.twig` template would look like if we put all of these codes in it. So, another reason to keep the base template short and tidy is increasing readability. As you will see in the final code, some of these blocks will be moved to separate files and included where they are needed. This way, they will be even more organized.

As you may have noticed, the previous template is optimized for each environment. If we are in the development environment, then we need to be able to deal with each asset individually. For example, we might need to update a class in a css file or add a new function to a js file. However, when we are in the production environment, then performance is critical. So, compiling ten assets into one file and loading it once is way faster than loading ten individual files. This is one of the assetic features:

```
{% if app.environment == 'prod' %}
        {# Compile all JS into 1 file #}
        {% javascripts
                '@jquery'
                '@bootstrap_js'
                output='js/compiled/main.js' %}
            <script src="{{ asset_url }}"></script>
        {% endjavascripts %}
```

Is there any way to get rid of those conditional blocks and define the environment-related conditions somewhere else? Yes, there is. Open the `config.yml` file and notice the following lines in it:

```
# mava/app/config/config.yml
assetic:
    debug:          '%kernel.debug%'
    use_controller: '%kernel.debug%'
```

The `debug` option here gets the environment and, based on the current environment, decides to combine or not to combine assets. In other words, we don't need to add a conditional block to our templates. So the template can be refactored as follows:

```
{% extends "base.html.twig" %}
{% block title 'MAVA' %}
{% block head %}
    <link rel="icon" sizes="16x16" href="{{ asset('favicon.ico') }}" />
        {% stylesheets
        '@bootstrap_css'
        '@mava_css'
        output='css/compiled/main.css' %}
```

```
        <link rel="stylesheet" href="{{ asset_url }}" />
        {% endstylesheets %}
{% endblock %}
{% block javascripts %}
        {% javascripts
        '@jquery'
        '@bootstrap_js'
        output='js/compiled/main.js' %}
        <script src="{{ asset_url }}"></script>
        {% endjavascripts %}
{% endblock %}
```

You might ask what `bootstrap_js` and `bootstrap_css` is. I will answer this question soon. For now, be aware that they belong to the frontend framework that we will use in this project.

To navigate or not to navigate

Before the JavaScript block, there are other three blocks in the base template that are not defined in `mava_base.html.twig`; why?

Well, this is part of our templating strategy. Mava is a web application and not a website. This means that we might have some pages that follow a completely different structure and contain different types of elements. For example, in the login page, I don't want to show the navigation bar. This becomes very handy when our visitors are using a mobile device. Removing the navigation and footer from the login page makes it look more like a mobile app.

This means that we can extend `mava_base.html.twig` for special pages, yet we need another template (containing navigation, footer, and so on) for pages with a default structure. So, create another template in the same place as the other two and add the following content to it:

```
{# app/Resources/views/default.html.twig #}
{% extends "mava_base.html.twig" %}
{% block navigation %}
    {% include "navigations.html.twig" %}
{% endblock %}
```

There you have it. As you can see, a lot of clutter has been removed simply by organizing blocks in their own files. Now we can extend `mava_base.html.twig` for special pages and `default.html.twig` for normal pages and, thanks to the `include` tag, it will include the navigation blocks automatically. Here is a visual representation of what we have created so far (each color represents a `twig` file):

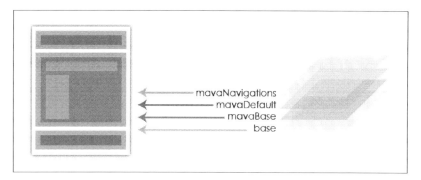

According to this structure, we need to create one more file that contains all the navigation. We will come back to that after creating the code for the first menu.

What is Bootstrap?

Look at the `mava_base.html.twig` file and you will notice that we mentioned bootstrap twice. Once it was mentioned in the head block and the other time, it was referenced in the JavaScript block. Bootstrap is a frontend framework that was created by Mark Otto and Jacob Thornton on Twitter. It contains a set of tools that makes responsive design and development a breeze. In August 2011, Twitter released Bootstrap as an open source project and since then, it has been one of the most popular repositories on GitHub. Any good web application needs to be accessible on mobile devices as well. So we are going to utilize the Bootstrap framework and make the `mava` project mobile-friendly.

MopaBootstrapBundle

There are a couple bundles that integrate Bootstrap into Symfony projects. `MopaBootstrapBundle` is one of the popular and stable bundles available. In this section, we will see how to install and configure this bundle in our project.

To process styles, I'm going to use Less. It is a CSS preprocessor that adds loads of functionality to styles. So, before installing `MopaBootstrapBundle`, make sure that you have familiarized yourself with Less and installed the latest version of it already:

```
$ npm install -g less
```

Check your installation via the following command:

```
$ lessc -v
lessc 2.6.1 (Less Compiler) [JavaScript]
```

Now install the bootstrap bundle and its dependencies via composer:

```
//composer.json
{
    "require": {
        "mopa/bootstrap-bundle": "dev-master",
        "twbs/bootstrap": "dev-master",

        "knplabs/knp-paginator-bundle": "dev-master"

    }
}

$ sudo
  composer install
```

 At the time of writing this chapter, the dev-master version of the preceding packages are the only branches that work fine with Symfony 3 and have no conflicts with other packages. If you received an error during installation, you might want to use the latest stable version of some packages instead.

Of course, using dev-master is not recommended if you are not a seasoned developer looking for cutting-edge features. However, for the time being, it is the only option.

Activate these bundles in the kernel:

```
// app/AppKernel.php
public function registerBundles()
{
    return array(
        // ...
        new Mopa\Bundle\BootstrapBundle\MopaBootstrapBundle(),
        new Knp\Bundle\PaginatorBundle\KnpPaginatorBundle(),
```

```
        // ...
    );
}
```

Bootstrap configuration

There are two important steps in configuration. First, we need to create symbolic links for Less:

```
$ bin/console mopa:bootstrap:symlink:less
Initializing composer ... done.
Checking symlink ... not existing
Creating symlink: /var/www/packt/mava/vendor/mopa/bootstrap-bundle/
Mopa/Bundle/BootstrapBundle/Resources/public/bootstrap
for target: ../../../../../../../twbs/bootstrap ... OK
```

The output of the previous command says that a new symbolic link to all bootstrap resources (fonts, styles, js, and others) was created in a subdirectory structure ending with `^/twbs/bootstrap`.

But where is this folder?

Secondly, symbolic fonts and web icons play a critical role in any bootstrap framework. As you may know, Glyphicons and FontAwesome are two famous font packages with all of those cool icons in them. I have included the latest version of FontAwesome (4.x) in this project. You can install this and the default Glyphicons by running the following commands:

```
$ bin/console assets:install
```

```
$ bin/console mopa:bootstrap:install:font
```

 Note that running the preceding command installs the default fonts that come with the Mopa bundle, which is the FontAwesome series. If you have other font requirements for your projects, you can easily install them as normal assets. In other words, just create a `/font` folder in the app/Resources directory and copy the font files over there. The next time you run the `assets:install` command, they will be installed in the `/web` directory and will be available to your project.

In the end, dump all assets to make sure that everything is up to date:

```
$ bin/console assetic:dump
```

Now you can benefit from all these new resources in your template simply by adding the following lines to `config.yml`:

```
#app/config/config.yml
#...
mopa_bootstrap:
    form: ~   # Adds twig form theme  support
    menu: ~   # enables twig helpers for menu
```

> Before moving on, make sure that there is no broken link to bootstrap references. If you go to `web/bundles/mopabootstrap`, you will find a file with symbolic links to the real bootstrap folder. It is critical to make sure that they are pointing to the right folder; otherwise, your template won't show properly:
>
> `bootstrap -> ../../../vendor/twbs/bootstrap/.`

While we are in the `config.yml` file, let's have a look at the assetic section. As I mentioned before, `AsseticBundle` works with two concepts, filters and assets:

```
# Assetic Configuration
assetic:
    debug:           "%kernel.debug%"
    use_controller: false
    bundles:         [ ]
    filters:
        cssrewrite: ~
        less:
            node: /usr/bin/node
            node_paths: [/usr/local/lib/node_modules]
            apply_to: "\.less$"
    assets:
        mava_css:
            inputs:
                - %kernel.root_dir%/Resources/public/css/mava.css
            filters:
                - less
                - cssrewrite
            output: css/mava.css
```

This is not the full configuration for our project and you can find it in the repository, but here we can see `filters` and `assets` entries. Under filters, there are two filters: `cssrewrite` and `less`.

Less is very well-documented, but rewriting css is a little tricky. There is not much information about it out there. What it does is basically create a better css file by rewriting parts of your original file. Why do we need this? Assetic generates new URLs for your assets and breaks all relative paths in the original CSS files. To fix this problem, we use the `cssrewrite` filter, which parses the CSS files and modifies the paths to reflect the new location.

Look at the `mava_css` entry under the `assets` section. It gets `app/Resources/public/mava.css` as input, applies less and `cssrewrite` filters to it, and saves it as `web/css/mava.css`. As we gave it a name in `config.yml`, it is very easy to access this asset just by calling its name. For example, in `mava_base.html.twig`, we accessed it by calling `@mava_css`.

Creating your first menu

Let's see how to create a bootstrap style menu. The menu feature of MopaBootstrapBundle is totally handled by KnpMenuBundle. Here are the required steps to create a menu:

1. Go to your AppBundle and create a new folder called `Menu`.

2. Add a new class and name it `Builder.php`; the contents of this class should be as follows:

```php
<?php
// mava/src/AppBundle/Menu/Builder.php
namespace Mava\CoreBundle\Menu;
use Knp\Menu\FactoryInterface;
use Symfony\Component\DependencyInjection\ContainerBuilder;

class Builder extends ContainerBuilder
{
    public function topMenu(FactoryInterface $factory, array $options)
    {
        $menu = $factory->createItem('root');
        $menu->setChildrenAttribute('class', 'nav navbar-top-links navbar-right');

        $dropdown2 = $menu->addChild(' ', array(
            'icon' => 'bell',
            'dropdown' => true,
            'caret' => true,
```

```
        ));

        // Create a dropdown header
        $dropdown2->addChild('notifications', array('dropdown-
header' => true))
            ->setAttribute('divider_append', true);

        // Create a dropdown with a caret
        $dropdown = $menu->addChild('', array(
            'icon' => 'user',
            'dropdown' => true,
            'caret' => true,
        ));

        // Create a dropdown header
        $dropdown->addChild('Edit Profile', array('route' =>
'sonata_user_profile_edit'));
        $dropdown->addChild('Change Password', array('route' =>
'sonata_user_change_password'));
        $dropdown->addChild('Logout', array('route' => 'sonata_
user_security_logout'));
        return $menu;
    }
```

Each public method that you add to this class represents a menu that you can call in your templates. Here, for example, I started a menu that I am going to show on top of the `topMenu()` page.

There are two ways that you can define attributes for each menu item. You can define them by calling a separate method:

```
$menu->setChildrenAttribute(
        'class',
        'nav navbar-top-links navbar-right'
);
```

In this example, we defined three classes for the `<ul>` element of the menu.

The other way is to define everything we need in an array where we add a menu item:

```
// Create a dropdown with a caret
$dropdown = $menu->addChild('', array(
    'icon' => 'user',
    'dropdown' => true,
    'caret' => true,
));
```

In the preceding example, we defined the menu option as a drop-down menu with a user icon and a little caret as a helper. This means that we can create submenus simply by defining a new child for a current child as follows:

```
// Create a dropdown header
$dropdown->addChild('Edit Profile', array('route' => 'sonata_user_
profile_edit'));
```

 This menu option points to the route to edit a profile. You can find the real URI by running the following command:
`$ app/console router:debug  sonata_user_profile_edit`

Rendering the menu in a template

Now it is time to create `navigations.html.twig` and render our menu in it. Go to `app/Resources/views` and create this file with the following content:

```
<!-- /.navbar-header -->
{{ mopa_bootstrap_menu('AppBundle:Builder:topMenu') }}
<div class="navbar-default sidebar" role="navigation">
{# a place holder for future side menu
    <div class="sidebar-nav navbar-collapse">
 {{ mopa_bootstrap_menu('AppBundle:Builder:sideMenu') }}
    </div>
#}
</div>
```

The `mopa_bootstrap_menu()` command drills down to the `AppBundle/Menu/Builder.php` class and calls the `topMenu()` method. Based on the contents available in this method, it will render the menu and its options.

 As you can see, I have added a sideMenu to this template too. The logic is the same and you can check out the GitHub repository for the `sideMenu()` method in `Builder.php` and the complete source for the navigation template.

The Dashboard template

With all important pieces in place, it is now time to use the Bootstrap framework and make our project look pretty. To make your life easier, you can start with the base template that comes with MopaBootstrapBundle and modify it the way you like.

However, if you are after that professional slick look for your dashboard, you can use a free template and build your website on top of that. There are so many resources that offer professional templates. Some good places to start are www. `startbootstrap.com` and `html5up.net`. This becomes very handy specially when you don't have many creative or design skills.

To start, let's see how to use the default template (the one with navigations) in our pages. Go to `app/Resources/views/dashboard/index.html.twig` and replace the content with the following:

```twig
{% extends "AppBunlde:Dashboard:default.html.twig" %}
{% block mavaBody %}
    <div id="page-wrapper">
        <div class="row">
            place holder
        </div>
        <!-- /.row -->
    </div>
{% endblock %}
```

Now visit the `/dashboard` page and you will see that it works. There are two menus, top and side, and a placeholder for the dashboard contents. What happened is simple; we just inherited what has been defined in `default.html.twig` and displayed its contents on the dashboard page:

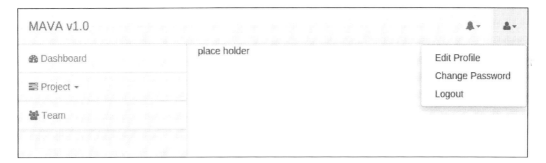

The good news is that this template is fully responsive. Resize your browser window and see it yourself.

As you can see, the user menu has three options. Implementing the **Logout** option is simple; we just need to point the URI element of this option to the logout path. However, **Edit Profile** and **Change Password** options are engaged to `SonataUserBundle` templates. The question is how to integrate our own template into a third-party bundle.

Overriding templates

In order to override a template that ships with a third-party bundle (such as `SonataUserBundle`), we have to create a duplicate of it in the `app/Resources` folder and modify it here.

To see how it works, let's start with the login page. At the moment, it looks ugly and empty and covered with some unnecessary elements.

Copy a few folders from `sonata-project` to your `app/Resources` folder as follows:

```
$ mkdir app/Resources/SonataUserBundle

$ cp -r vendors/sonata-project/user-bundle/Resources/views/
app/Resources/SonataUserBundle/
```

Now edit `Security/base_login.html.twig` as follows:

```
{# app/Resources/SonataUserBundle/views/Security/base_login.html.twig
#}
{% extends '::mavaBase.html.twig' %}
{% block mavaBody %}
    {% block fos_user_content %}
        {# rest of the template #}
    {% endblock %}
{% endblock %}
```

Here, you can see the benefit of saving blocks in separate files. As it is extended from the `mava_base` template, no menu will be shown, which is what we want. Visit the login page and you will see that the template matches the rest of the project.

Profile-related templates

I agree. Chasing every single template and extending them from what we want is not a pleasant thing to do. Luckily, we don't need to do this. Instead, just extend the layout in the root of the `views/` folder and, because everything in `views/` depends on it, the rest of the tribe will adapt the change:

```
{# app/Resources/SonataUserBundle/views/layout.html.twig #}
{%  extends '::default.html.twig' %}
```

There are still a few things that you need to do in order to fully customize the profile-related templates. For example, select the **User | Edit Profile** option from the dashboard and look at the resulting page:

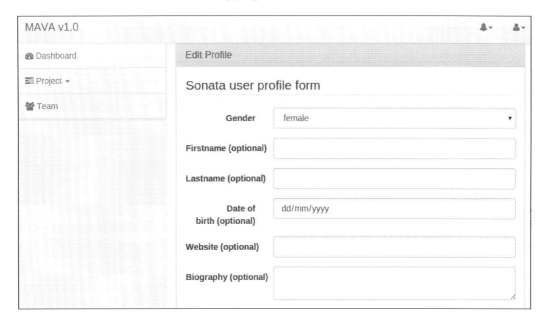

First of all, the title **Sonata user profile form** doesn't look very nice in our form. So, we need to get rid of it or replace it with our choice. Secondly, we might want to override the form field and modify (add, edit, or delete) the way that suits us best. More importantly, we need to add additional fields such as a photo for each user.

It sounds like a handful of changes and definitely needs some unit and acceptance tests. The completed test files are included in the GitHub repository:

```
https://github.com/Soolan/mava-project.git
```

Overriding forms is a three-step process. First, we have to create the forms that we want in our bundle. Then, we have to define them as a service. When this is done, we have to tell Sonata which form it should use. The same approach applies to any form (registration, profile edit, password change, and so on). To save some space, we are not going to add codes for all forms here and you can see some of the overridden forms in the mava project by referring to this project's GitHub repository:

```
git@github.com:Soolan/mava-project.git
```

To give you an example, imagine that we want to edit biography, first name, and last name in the edit profile form. Here is the process for this:

1. Go to `mava/src/AppBundle/Form` and create a new form as follows:

```php
<?php

namespace AppBundle\Form;

use Symfony\Component\Form\AbstractType;
use Symfony\Component\Form\FormBuilderInterface;
use Symfony\Component\OptionsResolver\OptionsResolver;

class ProfileType extends AbstractType
{
    public function buildForm(FormBuilderInterface $builder, array $options)
    {
        $builder
            ->add('firstname', null, array(
                'label'    => 'form.label_firstname',
                'required' => true
            ))
            ->add('lastname', null, array(
                'label'    => 'form.label_lastname',
                'required' => true
            ))
            ->add('biography', 'textarea', array(
                'label'    => 'form.label_biography',
                'required' => true
            ));
    }

    public function configureOptions(OptionsResolver $resolver)
    {
        $resolver->setDefaults(array(
            'data_class' => 'AppBundle\Entity\User',
            'intention'  => 'profile',
            'label' => 'Edit Profile'
        ));
    }

    public function getName()
    {
        return 'mava_user_profile';
    }
}
```

2. As you can see, the form legend can be edited in the `configureOptions()` method. Now define a service for it:

```
# mava/app/config/services.yml
services:
    mava_user.profile.form.type:
        class:
            AppBundle\Form\ProfileType
        tags:
            - { name: form.type, alias: mava_user_profile }
```

3. Now, let Symfony know about this new service by modifying `config.yml` as follows:

```
# mava/app/config/config.yml
sonata_user:
    # ...
    profile:
        form:
            type:     mava_user_profile
    #...
```

That's it. If you select the **Edit Profile** option again, you will see the modified version of this form.

Adding a profile photo is a little tricky and requires installing another Sonata bundle called `SonataMediaBundle`. I will show you how to do this in the next chapter.

Changing the backend logo

You probably want to put your own project's name and logo on the backend as well. Currently, it shows the Sonata project logo and the title **Sonata Admin** in front of it.

To do so, copy your logo file in `app/Resources/public/img/mava_logo.png`.

Then, install your assets:

```
$ bin/console assets:install
```

Now you can change your project's logo by adding the following lines to the `config.yml` file:

```
# app/config/config.yml
sonata_admin:
    title:       MAVA v1.0
    title_logo:  img/mava_logo.png
```

Log in to the administrator area and you will notice the new logo here:

Summary

In this chapter, we installed MopaBootstrapBundle to integrate the Bootstrap features into our Symfony project and created menus and rendered them in our template. We saw how to use assetic to manage assets and apply filters to them. You also learned how to override templates shipped with other vendors.

Bootstrap still has a lot to offer, and we will see how to use forms and collections to decorate each part of the dashboard in the next chapter. We will also see how to use JavaScript libraries (for example, `morris.js`) to create graphs.

8
Project Review

Let's improve the project a little. In this chapter, we are going to review what we have created so far and modify or add some more features to it. Our focus will be on the dashboard page where you can get a glimpse of what's going on in your current workspace. There will be reports for tasks and people whom tasks are assigned to. A notification system is a new feature that we will build in this chapter. It will alert us about the changes and overall progress of the project.

We will implement a commenting system as well. This is where team members add comments and reply to them for each task. This means that we need another entity with some one-to-many relationships to tasks and members.

In the real world, we should be able to upload files for each task. So, attachments will be another feature in this chapter and we will see how to use SonataMediaBundle to achieve this goal.

The dashboard's contents

The dashboard is a critical page. This is where we get an idea about the interaction between projects, members, and tasks in the current workspace. It should carry enough elements to provide a quick report about the activities that are happening in the application and, at the same time, it should be light enough to keep the loading time reasonably short.

For our MVP purposes, I would say that the following items should be enough:

- A block showing the number of new comments on tasks
- A block showing the number of due tasks
- A block showing the number of recently created tasks
- A block showing the number of completed tasks

- A notification panel showing the last seven events (notifications)
- A graph representing the visual progress of the current project

According to these blocks, the finished dashboard page will look like the following image:

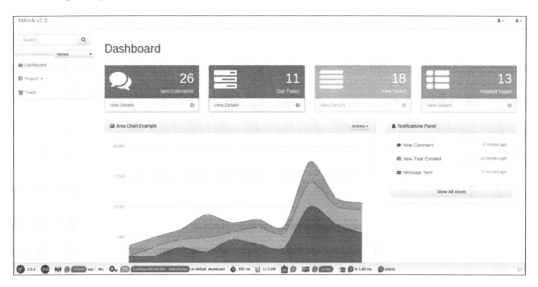

Visual blocks that provide statistics about tasks

Looking at the top blocks, three of them are dealing with tasks. What we are going to do is create one feature file for one of these blocks and ask Behat to generate the blueprints for the implementation. After having a clear direction to go in, we will create the unit tests. Finally, with all the functional and unit tests in place, we will start development.

This will be the strategy for every single development challenge in this chapter. However, to save some space, I will not copy every single bit of code here. You can find the finished code in the v0.1.8 release tag in the main GitHub repository. Instead, we are going to talk about concepts and strategies.

A feature file for the finished tasks block

Let's start by implementing the finished tasks block. This block represents the number of completed tasks. So, we can see where we are standing in the current project's progress by looking at the statistics provided in this block. Create a new feature file named `dashboard.feature` in your `/features` folder and add the following content to it:

```
# /features/dashboard.feature
@userDashboard
Feature: dashboard blocks
  In order to see my finished tasks
  As a user
  I am able to see finished task block in the dashboard

  @javascript
  Scenario: showing the finished task block in the dashboard
    Given I log in as Jack
    And I visit "/dashboard"
    Then the response status code should be 200
    And I should see "Finished Tasks!"
```

Who is Jack? He is simply a test user that can be generated via fixtures (refer to *Chapter 2*, *Request/Response life cycle*) or the following command (where we define the username, e-mail, and plain password for our new user):

```
$ bin/console fos:user:create Jack jack@mava.info jackpass --env=test
```

The next question would be how can we check whether a user has been logged in? Let's run Behat and generate the code snippet to answer this question:

```
bin/behat --tags="userDashboard" --append-snippets
```

 Yes, you can add a name annotation at the beginning of your feature file (that is, `@userDashboard`) and later use it as a tag in the command line (that is, `--tag="userDashboard"`). Only features or scenarios with the matching tag will be executed.

As you can see, we have an undefined scenario in the output with four steps:

```
1 scenario (1 undefined)
4 steps (2 undefined, 2 skipped)
```

All you need to do is open the `/features/bootstrap/FeaturesContext.php` file and modify the `Given` steps as follows:

```php
/**
 * @Given I  log in as Jack
 */
public function iLogInAsJack()
{
    $this->visit('/login');
    $this->fillField('username', 'Jack');
    $this->fillField('password', 'jackpass');
    $this->pressButton('_submit');
}

/**
 * @Given I visit :arg1
 */
public function iVisit($arg1)
{
    $this->visit($arg1);
}
```

Run the test and normally, it should fail. This means that we need to implement the template for the pages we are interested in.

If you have installed the template from the previous chapter (or you have checked out the chapter08 branch from the original GitHub repository), rerun the test and it should be all green:

```
Feature: dashboard blocks
  In order to see my finished tasks
  As a user
  I am able to see finished task block in the dashboard

  Scenario: showing the finished task block in the dashboard #
features/dashboard.feature:7
    Given I am logged in as Jack                              # Feature
Context::iAmLoggedInAsJack()
    And I visit "/dashboard"                                  #
FeatureContext::iVisit()
    Then the response status code should be 200               # Feature
Context::assertResponseStatus()
    And I should see "Finished Tasks!"                        # Feature
Context::assertPageContainsText()

1 scenario (1 passed)
4 steps (4 passed)
0m1.41s (21.29Mb)
```

You might ask that we didn't implement the `Then` step, then how do our tests check for status code `200`? If you look at steps three and four in the test results, you will see that there are two `assert` methods called. The first one checks the status code and the second one checks to see whether our desired text (in this scenario, `"Finished Tasks!"`) is available on this page.

As we are extending MinkContext, a lot of features (including checking for the `Then` step) come out of the box and we don't need to worry about them.

> A word of caution to readers who use the `@javascript` tag and want to see their browsers open the login page automatically, fill in the user and password fields, and press the submit button. Well, it does all of this without any problems, but when it opens the dashboard page—in case you are using the selenium2 driver—it cannot check for status code. So it fails that step and consequently skips the last step. Here is the error:
>
> Status code is not available from `Behat\Mink\Driver\` `Selenium2Driver (Behat\Mink\Exception\` `UnsupportedDriverActionException)`

Implementing the finished tasks block

So far, we have an empty shell for the functionality that we are interested in. Now, it is time to create some (failing) unit tests to find `"Finished Tasks"`. Let's say that we have a workspace with two projects in it and there are three finished tasks in both the projects combined. So what we need to do is assert the finished tasks and make sure that the total number is three. The finished tasks are shown in the dashboard area so, presumably, our unit test should be created for the dashboard controller:

```
// place holder for unit test codes
```

In order to define various statuses for tasks, we can add a new property to the task entity and name it `status`:

```
// src/AppBundle/Entity/Task.php
/**
 * @var string
 *
 * @ORM\Column(name="status", type="string", nullable=false)
 */
private $status;
```

Make sure that the database gets updated after every change:

```
$ bin/console doctrine:schema:update --force
```

After this, define three possible values to it: new, in progress and completed:

```
// src/AppBundle/Form/TaskType.php
public function buildForm(FormBuilderInterface $builder, array
$options)
    {
        $builder
            // … rest of task form
            ->add('status', ChoiceType::class, array(
                'choices' => array('new' => 'new',
                            'in progress' => 'in progress',
                        'completed' => 'completed'),
            ));
    }
```

Now with the new setup in place, simply create a new method in the task repository that is in charge of finding tasks with a completed status:

```
// src/AppBundle/Entity/TaskRepository
    public function finishedTasks($projectId){
        $q = $this->createQueryBuilder('t')
            ->where('t.project = :projectId')
            ->andWhere('t.status = :completed')
            ->setParameter('projectId', $projectId)
          ->setParameter('completed', 'completed')
            ->getQuery();
        return $q->getResult();
    }
```

Looks simple but something is missing here. It finds all the finished tasks in a particular project. This means that we have to choose a project first and then use this method for that particular project only.

What if we needed to see all the finished tasks in the current workspace? In other words, if we have defined four different projects in the current workspace and each project has a couple of finished tasks, then we need to find them all and show them in the finished task block.

The question is should we find them via the Project repository or is it better to query them via the Task repository? The answer is both. We need two methods here. From the Project side of the story—given that the workspace ID is provided—we need to find all the projects that share the same workspace:

```
// src/AppBundle/Entity/ProjectRepository
    public function getAllProjects($workSpaceId){
        $q = $this->createQueryBuilder('p')
```

```
            ->where('p.workspace = :workSpaceId')
            ->setParameter('workSpace_id', $workSpaceId)
            ->getQuery();
        return $q->getResult();
    }
```

Now that we have got the projects, we can look into each of them via the task repository and find all the finished tasks.

This is what the getFinishedTasks() method does for us:

```
    public function getFinishedTasks($projectId){
        $q = $this->createQueryBuilder('t')
            ->where('t.project = :projectId')
            ->andWhere('t.status = :completed')
            ->setParameter('projectID', $projectId)
            ->setParameter('completed', 'completed')
            ->getQuery();
        return $q->getResult();
    }
```

All we need now is a mechanism to count all the finished tasks and add up all of them. We can create a utility method for this. In AppBundle, create a new folder, call it Util, and add the following class to it:

```
<?php
namespace AppBundle\Util;
use Doctrine\ORM\EntityManagerInterface;
class Mava {
    private $em;
    public function __construct(EntityManagerInterface $em)
    {
        $this->em = $em;
    }
}
```

The Mava utility class is going to manage a couple of entity requests. That's why we have to initialize an EntityManagerInterface object in the constructor. Now let's create a new method to find all the finished tasks in the current workspace:

```
public function finishedTasks($wsId)
{
    $projects = $this->getAllProjects($wsId);
    $taskRepo = $this->em->getRepository('CoreBundle:Task');
    $total = 0;
    foreach ($projects as $project){
```

```
        $total += count($taskRepo->
            getFinishedTasks($project->getId()));
    }
    return $total;
}
public function wsAllProjects($wsID){
    return $this->em
        ->getRepository('CoreBundle:Project')
        ->getAllProjects($wsID);
}
```

As you can see, we refer to the Project repository to find all the projects in the current workspace first. Then, for each project, we refer to the Task repository to find all the tasks with a `completed` status.

Implementing the dashboard controller

It is good to have a utility class full of helper methods to do what we need to be done. This way, we take the functionality out of the controllers and keep them lean and clean.

To use the utility methods though, the best practice is to define them as a service. Don't worry about the details of how it is done and what happens behind the scene. I will explain the service mechanism with details in the next chapter. For now, add the following service definition to your CoreBundle:

```
{# /src/AppBundle/Resources/config/services.yml #}
services:
    mava_util:
        class: AppBundle\Util\Mava
        arguments: ['@doctrine.orm.entity_manager']
```

Now we can access this service in the controller just by getting its name:

```
<?php
namespace AppBundle\Controller;
use Symfony\Bundle\FrameworkBundle\Controller\Controller;
class DashboardController extends Controller
{
    public function indexAction($ws=null)
    {
        // ...
        $util = $this->get('mava_util');
        $finishedTasks = $util->FinishedTasks($ws);
```

```
        // ...
        return $this->render(
         'CoreBundle:Dashboard:index.html.twig', array(
            'finishedTasks' => $finishedTasks,
        ));
    }
}
```

We have access to all methods in our utility class simply by calling $this->get('mava_util'), so we can call FinishedTasks() and pass the total number of finished tasks in the current workspace to the template for the rendering.

In the template, all we need to do is receive this parameter and print it out in the proper bock:

```
{# src/AppBundle/Resources/views/Dashboard/index.html.twig #}
    {# … #}
            <div class="row">
                <div class="col-xs-3">
                    <i class="fa fa-th-list fa-5x"></i>
                </div>
                <div class="col-xs-9 text-right">
                    <div class="huge">{{ finishedTasks }}</div>
                    <div>Finished Tasks!</div>
                </div>
            </div>
    {# … #}
```

The same workflow applies to other task blocks (that is, New Tasks and Due Tasks). You can find the completed utility code, Dashboard controller, and Dashboard template in the repository.

Uploading files with SonataMediaBundle

There are a couple of places where we need to upload files or images in our project. For example, some tasks have attachments (documents).

To deal with this requirement, I am going to introduce one of Sonata project's handy bundles, SonataMediaBundle, and embed its functionality into the mava project. To begin with, install, register, and do the required configurations in the same way explained on the www.sonata-project.org website.

Note that you need to install `SonataEasyExtendsBundle` as well to configure the entities properly. Depending on your current admin bundle version, this bundle may or may not be installed already. Check your `AppKernell.php`, and if you don't see the Easy Extends bundle here, this means that you have to install it before proceeding to generate Media entities.

 After installation and, if by any chance, you get an error regarding a dependency to `jms/serializer-bundle`, make sure that you install and register this bundle as well.

Here, you can find complete instructions on how to install and configure SonataMediaBundle:

`https://sonata-project.org/bundles/media/2-2/doc/index.html.`

Adding an attachment feature to the Task entity

With SonataMediaBundle in place, let's see how we can use it to attach files to tasks. First, modify the Task entity and change the attachment property as follows (to keep it simple, let's say that we need only one attachment per task for now):

```php
// src/AppBundle/Entity/Task.php
// …

/**
 * @ORM\OneToOne(targetEntity= "Application\Sonata\MediaBundle\Entity\
Media",cascade={"persist"})
 * @ORM\JoinColumn(name="attachment_id",referencedColumnName="id")
**/
protected $attachment;
```

As you can see, this property is pointing to another entity and will be saved as a column named `attachment_id`. That's how Doctrine handles the attachment for each Task.

Don't forget to update the database with the new changes:

```
$ bin/console doctrine:schema:update --force
```

Next, we need to update the Task form. Open `TaskType.php` and modify the attachment field as follows:

```
// src/AppBundle/Form/TaskType.php
<?php
// ...
class TaskType extends AbstractType
{
    /**
     * @param FormBuilderInterface $builder
     * @param array $options
     */
    public function buildForm(FormBuilderInterface $builder, array
$options)
    {
        $builder
            // ...
            ->add('attachment', 'sonata_media_type', array(
                'provider' => 'sonata.media.provider.file',
                'context'  => 'default'
            ))
            // ...
            ));
    }
}
```

Now, if you visit `/admin/task/new`, you will see a fully functioning file upload field for attachments and you can check that files are uploaded under the `web/uploads/media` folder.

Team and team members

Usually, projects consist of several tasks and cannot be done by a single person. So, we need to introduce the concept of team and define relationships between **Team**, **User**, and **Project** entities in our application. The simplest definition for the **Team** entity could be: all the people who work on the same project. This means that we need to modify our current **User** entity and add a new property that defines the relationship between **Team** and **User**.

The Team entity

The following image shows the relationship between **Team**, **Project**, and **User** entities. To keep it simple, let's say that each User can be a member of one Team only and there is only one team for each project:

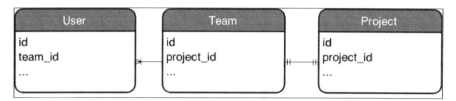

With the MVP approach in mind and considering the preceding image, the Team entity can be defined as follows:

```php
<?php
class Team
{
    /**
     * @var integer
     * @ORM\Column(name="id", type="integer")
     * @ORM\Id
     * @ORM\GeneratedValue(strategy="AUTO")
     */
    private $id;

    /**
     * @var string
     * @ORM\Column(name="Title", type="string", length=255)
     */
    private $title;

    /**
     * @var string
     * @ORM\Column(name="Description", type="text")
     */
    private $description;

    /**
     * @ORM\OneToOne(targetEntity="AppBundle\Entity\Project")
     * @ORM\JoinColumn(name="project_id", referencedColumnName="id")
     */
    protected $project;
//...
}
```

Now we need to update the User entity accordingly. So open it and add the team property and its getter and setter as follows:

```php
<?php
//...
class User extends BaseUser
{
    /**
     * @ORM\OneToOne(targetEntity="AppBundle\Entity\Team")
     * @ORM\JoinColumn(name="team_id", referencedColumnName="id")
     */
    protected $team;

    /**
     * Set team
     * @param \AppBundle\Entity\Team $team
     * @return Team
     */
    public function setTeam(\AppBundle\Entity\Team $team = null)
    {
        $this->team = $team;
        return $this;
    }

    /**
     * Get team
     * @return \AppBundle\Entity\Team
     */
    public function getTeam()
    {
        return $this->team;
    }
//...
```

 Note that the value of team for newly created users is null by default. This way, we don't get errors for new users or users who are not a member of any team.

This new property in the User entity is more than just a new bridge between entities. We will see how to use it to manage notifications and e-mails.

Adding the admin feature for the Team entity is the same as previous entities. Define the required admin class (that is, `/src/AppBundle/Admin/TeamAdmin.php`) and required forms and fields:

```php
<?php
namespace AppBundle\Admin;
use Sonata\AdminBundle\Admin\Admin;
use Sonata\AdminBundle\Datagrid\ListMapper;
use Sonata\AdminBundle\Datagrid\DatagridMapper;
use Sonata\AdminBundle\Form\FormMapper;
class TeamAdmin extends Admin
{
    // Fields to be shown on create/edit forms
    protected function configureFormFields(FormMapper $formMapper)
    {
        $formMapper
            ->add('title' , 'text')
            ->add('description', 'textarea')
            ->add('project','entity',
                array(
                    'class' => 'CoreBundle:Project',
                    'property' => 'title'
                ));
    }

    // Fields to be shown on filter forms
    protected function configureDatagridFilters(
        DatagridMapper $datagridMapper)
    {
        $datagridMapper
            ->add('title')
            ->add('description');
    }

    // Fields to be shown on lists
    protected function configureListFields(ListMapper $listMapper)
    {
        $listMapper
            ->addIdentifier('title')
            ->add('description');
    }
}
```

Then, add it as a service to your `admin.yml` file:

```
# src/AppBundle/Resources/config/admin.yml
services:
    # ...
    sonata.admin.team:
            class: CoreBundle\Admin\TeamAdmin
            tags:
{ name: sonata.admin, manager_type: orm,
group: "Content", label: "Team" }
            arguments:
                - ~
                - CoreBundle\Entity\Team
                - ~
            calls:
    [ setTranslationDomain, [CoreBundle]]
```

This way, we tell `SonataAdminBundle` that we need a new item under the `Content` group in order to manage our Team entities.

Adding a notification system

A notification system is a critical part in every task management application. We need to be informed about events that happen in the system. Here are a few examples of task notifications. Similar rules apply to projects, workspaces, teams, and users:

- When a new task is assigned
- When a new task is created
- When there is a new attachment for a task
- When there are some changes in a task
- When a task is completed

According to this business logic, all entities created so far are missing a crucial part. They all need a mechanism to keep track of two times: the first, the moment they have been created and second is the last time they have been updated.

In the following section, I will show you how to implement this mechanism for the Task entity. You can do the same for the rest of the entities or fetch the updated code from the `Chapter08` branch.

Adding time tracking properties

It would be very helpful if we could track the activities that happen in a Task entity. For example, sometimes we need to get the access time to a specific task in order to accomplish an other functionality in the dashboard area.

To find out when a new task has been created and the last time it was updated, we need to define new properties as follows:

```php
<?php
// src/AppBundle/Entity/Task.php
//...
/**
 * Task
 * ...
 * @ORM\HasLifecycleCallbacks()
 */
class Task
{
    //...
    /**
     * @var \DateTime
     * @ORM\Column(name="created_at", type="datetime")
     */
    protected $createdAt;

    /**
     * @var \DateTime
     * @ORM\Column(name="updated_at", type="datetime")
     */
    protected $updatedAt;
    /**
     * Sets the creation date
     * @ORM\PrePersist
     */
    public function setCreatedAt()
    {
        $this->createdAt = new \DateTime();
        $this->updatedAt = new \DateTime();
    }

    /**
     * Returns the creation date
     * @return \DateTime
     */
```

```php
    public function getCreatedAt()
    {
        return $this->createdAt;
    }


    /**
     * Sets the last update date
     * @ORM\PreUpdate
     */
    public function setUpdatedAt()
    {
        $this->updatedAt = new \DateTime();
    }


    /**
     * Returns the last update date
     * @return \DateTime
     */
    public function getUpdatedAt()
    {
        return $this->updatedAt;
    }
```

As you can see, there is nothing special about it. Just new properties with slightly different getters and setters. However, you may have noticed that they are defined as protected and there are some new annotations as well.

Let's start with the annotations: `@ORM\HasLifeCycleCallbacks()`, `@ORM\PreUpdate`, and `@ORM\PrePersist` are telling Doctrine that we want to use your internal event system.

Yes, Doctrine comes with a fast event system that can handle some common tasks for us. For example, `@ORM\PrePersist` means run the methods mentioned by this annotation before flushing the queries and inserting new records into the table. However, `@ORM\PreUpdate` fires an event to update the current records only.

In our case, when we create a new Task, the `CreatedAt` and `UpdatedAt` properties are set to the current time, and when an available record is modified, only the `UpdatedAt` property will get a new value.

Using Doctrine's event system keeps our controllers a little cleaner. Imagine if you wanted to take care of the creation and update times yourself. You have to create a few extra methods for them and call them every time they are needed.

You can find more details about Doctrine's events at the following link:

`http://doctrine-orm.readthedocs.org/en/latest/reference/events.html`

 If you are looking to add more advanced behaviors to your entities, then using Doctrine extensions is the answer: `http://symfony.com/doc/current/cookbook/doctrine/common_extensions.html`.

Before proceeding to the next topic, don't forget to update your tables:

```
bin/console doctrine:schema:update --force
```

The notification business logic

The whole idea for notifications is for them to be generated automatically by the system. This means that for most of db queries, the system should generate a notification automatically and alert the user(s) who are involved to that event.

The Notifications class concerns users only, so the basic properties for the Notification entity would be as follows:

```php
<?php
namespace AppBundle\Entity;
use Doctrine\ORM\Mapping as ORM;

/**
 * Notification
 * @ORM\Table(name="notification")
 * @ORM\Entity(repositoryClass= "AppBundle\Entity\
NotificatioRepository")
 */
class Notification
{
    /**
     * @var integer
     * @ORM\Column(name="id", type="integer")
     * @ORM\Id
     * @ORM\GeneratedValue(strategy="AUTO")
     */
    private $id;

    /**
     * @var string
```

```
    * @ORM\Column(name="subject", type="string", length=45)
    */
   private $subject;

   /**
    * @var string
    * @ORM\Column(name="body", type="text", nullable=true)
    */
   private $body;

   /**
    * @var \AppBundle\Entity\User
    * @ORM\ManyToOne(targetEntity="AppBundle\Entity\User")
    * @ORM\JoinColumn(name="user_id", referencedColumnName="id")
    */
   private $user;

   /**
    * @var \DateTime
    * @ORM\Column(name="created_at", type="datetime")
    */
   protected $createdAt;

   /**
    * @var \DateTime
    * @ORM\Column(name="updated_at", type="datetime")
    */
   protected $updatedAt;

   //... and related setters and getters
}
```

As we want this entity to be generated automatically, the usual controllers won't be very helpful here. We need something more extensible. A mechanism that automates the process without our intervention. We still can do it in the controller way but let's develop a service to deal with the heavy lifting for us.

If you recall from the previous topic, Doctrine's event system was in charge of creating and updating times for the Task entity. So we can benefit from the same mechanism for our personal matters. This means that if we create some services and hook them to Doctrine events (that is, PrePersist, PostUpdate, and so on), then we can save tons of code.

So here is the plan. We have a couple of entities in our application. We will have an entity for notifications. We want to notify specific users about any change in our entities. The following image summarizes this business logic:

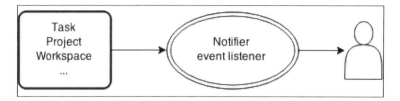

Events, event dispatchers, and event listeners

An event is simply a PHP object that carries some information. An event dispatcher is a mechanism that fires events. In our example, Doctrine has its own event system containing all predefined events and dispatchers, and an event listener is another class that is in charge of receiving events and reacting to them accordingly.

In our case, all we need to do is create a service to listen to these events. Let's start by defining a new service in AppBundle:

```
# src/AppBundle/Resources/config/services.yml
services:
    #...
    notification.listener:
      class: CoreBundle\EventListener\Notifier
      tags:
    { name: doctrine.event_listener, event: postPersist }
```

There are a couple of things to notice. First, we need to create a folder called EventListener and add a new class named Notifier to it. This class will be our event listener and, as you can see, we are interested in events called postPersist in the service settings.

So, we have to create a method in our EventListener class and name it after that event. This way, every time a postPersist event is fired by Doctrine, our method is ready to catch it and do something about it.

The Notifier event listener

The important thing about an event listener is that it will listen to all entities and cannot distinguish, say, the Task entity from the Project entity. It will be our job to deal with each event source separately. So add the following contents to `Notifier.php`:

```php
<?php
// src/AppBundle/EventListener/Notifier.php
namespace AppBundle\EventListener;
use Doctrine\ORM\Event\LifecycleEventArgs;
use Symfony\Component\HttpFoundation\Response;
use CoreBundle\Entity\Workspace;
use CoreBundle\Entity\Task;
use CoreBundle\Entity\Team;
use CoreBundle\Entity\Project;

class Notifier {
    private $subject;
    private $body;
    private $user;
    private $em;
    public function postPersist(LifecycleEventArgs $args)
    {
        $entity = $args->getEntity();
        $this->em = $args->getEntityManager();
        $this->notifyRelatedUsers($entity);
    }
    // ToDo: add methods for storing notifications
}
```

We used the `LifeCycleEventArgs` class here. The objects of that type provide methods to access an entity and entity manager. With the entity in our sight, the next step will be to recognize its type. So create another method in this class and add the following contents to it:

```php
<?php
// src/AppBundle/EventListener/Notifier.php
//...
class Notifier {
    //...
    public function notifyRelatedUsers($entity, $em)
    {
        if ($entity instanceof Task){
            $this->subject = $entity->getTitle();
```

```
            $this->body ="updates for task: ".$entity->getTitle();
            $this->user = $entity->getUser();
        }
        $this->addNewNotification();
    }
}
```

Here, we only checked for the easiest entity. Task is the easiest entity to deal with because it has a user property defined already.

If you look at other entities such as Workspace or Project, you will see that there is no user access in them. So what should we do? We have to cover every entity. For example, if there is a change in a project title or project due date, we need to notify people who are working on it, right?

To deal with this challenge, we can create methods to find users who are involved in a particular project or workspace and return the user ID. These methods can live in the entity repositories. They can also be defined in /src/AppBundle/Util/Mava.php and be accessed like a service. You can find the complete code for every single entity in this chapter's branch.

After finding the users who are involved in the current entity updates, the last step will be to add a new record to the notifications table:

```php
<?php
// src/AppBundle/EventListener/Notifier.php
//...
class Notifier {
    //...
    public function addNewNotification()
    {
        $manager = $this->em;
        $notification = new Notification();
        $notification->setSubject($this->subject);
        $notification->setBody($this->body);
        $notification->setUser($this->user);
        $manager->persist($notification);
        $manager->flush();
        return new Response('notification id '.$notification-
>getId().' successfully created');
    }
}
```

With all the notifications persisted in the database, when a user logs in to his account, we can fetch the notifications that match his user ID and show them to him. As you saw before, finding notifications by the user ID is a very simple thing to do and can be done through a method in the notification controller.

Summary

In this chapter, we reviewed the code developed in the past chapters and applied best Symfony practices to it. We saw how to turn ordinary code into services, do the required configurations for them, and call them whenever they are needed.

We introduced a few more entities for the project and created controllers and views for each of them using the BDD/TDD approach. We saw how to create event listeners as a service and how to benefit from Doctrine's event system in our project. The whole time, we let Jenkins orchestrate the development /test/ build life cycle for us.

In the next few chapters, our focus will be on Symfony services in detail and we will examine different techniques and use cases for them.

9
Services and Service Containers

Imagine that you are in charge of maintaining a legacy code and you find a couple of classes, with over 1,000 lines of code each, which have a long list of variables, constants, methods, and so on. What a mess; even reading that code takes ages, let alone understanding and maintaining it.

You might think, okay, I can break down those big classes into, say, 10 smaller ones and instantiate them in the main class. This helps a little, but it still wastes a lot of memory and, more importantly, it is hard to test and maintain them because they are tightly coupled to each other.

So what is the solution? The best way to deal with situations like this (or implementing a big project from scratch) is to read and understand the business requirements first and assemble a list of functionality for that application. Then, create one class for each functionality. It is totally fine if a feature consists of multiple functionality but before implementing that feature, create one single class for each simple functionality first. In other words, break down the logic to a point that it cannot be more simplified. This is essential and those classes can be considered as the building blocks of **Service-Oriented Architecture (SOA)** later. In the SOA architecture pattern, if you decide to modify or replace one of those building blocks with something else, it shouldn't interfere with the flow of the application or prevent the rest of the application from functioning.

This chapter is mainly about answering the following two questions:

1. How can we turn these classes into services?

2. How can we manage these services (that is, instantiate them and call their methods)?

How to create a service

You don't create services. You create classes and they are already SERVICES if they DO something.

So, the answer to the first question is simple: in reality, you don't need to do anything special to turn an object into a service. It needs only one aspect to be qualified as a service. It simply needs to do something. In other words, if a class contains methods that actually perform a task, you can call the object instantiated from that class a service. For example, Symfony entities are not services because they normally consist of a bunch of property definitions. However, any PHP object that takes these entities and performs some action on them can be called a service.

So, whenever you create a new class, you are potentially creating a new service. Service is just a fancy new name. That's all.

How are services beneficial to our projects?

If we are creating services in our professional lives (without realizing it), then why don't we feel any difference in our codes?

This is because classes are the body of a service. Without their souls, they are simply another PHP object. Their soul is the concept that gives them birth by instantiating them only if they are needed.

The Dependency Injection Container (or Service Container) is such a concept. It manages the instantiation of services on demand. This means that the service container constructs and returns them once if they are requested. This utilizes memory and application performance in two ways:

- If you create a service but never use it, no memory will be wasted for instantiation

- If you create a service and use it multiple times, memory will be allocated for the size of one instance only and will be shared across all the instances

This is powerful. Imagine the memory saved in this way.

What if we needed a unique instance of a service? In that case, we have to set the shared settings to `false` in the service definition:

```
services:
    some_service:
        class: some_class
        Shared: false
```

How to call a service

We have called a service in our project before. To know the answer, open `mava/src/AppBundle/Controller/DashboardController.php` and note two things:

```php
<?php
namespace AppBundle\Controller;
use Symfony\Bundle\FrameworkBundle\Controller\Controller;
class DashboardController extends Controller
{
    public function indexAction()
    {
        $uId = $this->getUser()->getId();
        $util = $this->get('mava_util');
        //...
    }
}
```

First, this class extends Symfony's `Controller` class. Secondly, spot the `get(mava_util)` method at line 9. This method is in charge of calling services and is defined in the `Controller.php` class as follows:

```php
/**
 * Gets a container service by its id.
 * @param string $id The service id
 * @return object The service
 */
public function get($id)
{
    //...
    return $this->container->get($id);
}
```

In this example, it calls the `mava_util` service and benefits from its methods. Moving the query logic into `mava_util` gives us the flexibility of accessing them anywhere in the project via a simple `get()` method. Besides, no matter how many times we call this service, it will occupy memory for one instantiation only and leave us with better utilized resources.

How to configure a service

In the previous topic, we got the `mava_util` service and used its methods to fetch user projects and tasks with various statuses. How does a service container construct a service? In other words, where are the configurations defined?

As developers, we give instructions on how to construct and return a service via the `config.yml` file. We can put the instructions directly in the `config.yml` file or somewhere else (that is, `services.yml`) and import them to `config.yml`.

Keep in mind that if you defined your services in a bundle, no further configuration is required and they will be loaded automatically. We will read more about this soon.

Open the `mava/src/AppBundle/resources/config/services.yml` file and note the definition for `mava_util`:

```
services:
    # ...
    mava_util:
        class: AppBundle\Util\Mava
        arguments: ['@doctrine.orm.entity_manager']
```

In this configuration, the class entry defines where the body of a service is located and arguments are a list of parameters that can be passed to that class while the service is being constructed. These parameters could be a simple string (or any other scalar value) or another service.

Why is it called a Dependency Injection Container?

You may have noticed that I used Service Container and Dependency Injection Container interchangeably. Based on what we have seen so far, the term Service Container makes sense: we have a couple of services and there is a container that manages them. Right?

However, what does it mean when we say Dependency Injection Container? Who injects what in this definition?

Look at the constructor in the `Mava.php` class again:

```
class Mava
{
    private $em;
    public function __construct(EntityManager $em)
    {
        $this->em = $em;
    }
    // ...
}
```

As you can see, we defined and initialized an `EntityManager` variable in its constructor and, if you look at the arguments for `mava_util` in `services.yml`, you will notice that it is actually a doctrine service called `entity_manager`:

```
mava_util:
    class: AppBundle\Util\Mava
    arguments: ['@doctrine.orm.entity_manager']
```

So basically, we have injected an `entity_manager` dependency into our `mava_util` service to benefit from its features. This is why it is sometimes called Dependency Injection Container.

This type of injection is called a constructor injection. Other types of injections are setter injection and property injection. You can read about these types and their pros and cons at the following link:

`http://symfony.com/doc/current/components/dependency_injection/types.html`.

Injecting services into other services is a very powerful idea. This means that you can use the power of other services in your services without worrying about memory usage, maintainability, and testability or being concerned about unreadable bulky code. You get the service(s) from the container whenever you want and however you want and, at the end, your Controllers stay lean and clean.

To recap, we need to do only two things to have a service up and running:

- A class that does something globally in our application
- A configuration file that tells the Service Container (Dependency Injection Container) how that service should be constructed

Of course, this configuration file has a lot of details and we can talk about it forever. Instead of repeating what has been explained in the official Symfony documentation, I'm going to expand on two more service examples that we have created for this application already. Before doing this, I would like to talk about another approach to load service configurations.

Why didn't we import services inside the bundle?

You may have noticed that we have a `service.yml` file in our `AppBundle` that is not imported to `config.yml`:

```
# app/config/config.yml
imports:
    - { resource: parameters.yml }
    - { resource: security.yml }
    - { resource: services.yml }      #app/config/services.yml
    - { resource: @AppBundle/Resources/config/admin.yml }
    { resource: sonata_classification.yml }
```

How come our `mava_util` service (which has been configured in `src/AppBundle/Resources/config/services.yml`) works?

Please bear in mind that there is nothing wrong with adding another resource line as follows:

```
    - { resource: @AppBundle/Resources/config/services.yml }
```

We are about to see another Symfony feature that makes bundles more decoupled.

When we generate a bundle with the Symfony console, a folder named `DependencyInjection` with the following classes is created:

```
AppBundle
    |- ...
    |_ DependencyInjection
            |- Configuration.php
            |_ AppExtension.php
```

The `AppExtension` class is the one that we are interested in. With this class, you can define all of your bundle configurations in the bundle itself and enable it to be loaded automatically wherever the bundle is used.

In other words, if you want to use this bundle in another project, simply copy the bundle in the `/src` folder and off you go. You don't need to worry about importing the service (or other) settings to `config.yml`.

Let's have a look in the `AppExtension` class and see how it works:

```php
<?php
namespace AppBundle\DependencyInjection;
//...
class AppExtension extends Extension
{
    public function load(array $configs,
                         ContainerBuilder $container)
    {
        $configuration = new Configuration();
        $config = $this->processConfiguration(
                                        $configuration,
                                        $configs
                                        );
        $loader = new Loader\YamlFileLoader($container, new
FileLocator(__DIR__.'/../Resources/config'));
        $loader->load('services.yml');
        $loader->load('admin.yml');
    }
}
```

As you can see, the `loader()` method does the trick. It simply loads all the `.yml` files available in the `Resources/config` folder of the bundle. This is why we don't need to import them to `app/config.yml`.

How to create and load services via autowiring

There are times when we only care about quick and dirty prototyping for a service. We don't know the service details and it is an ongoing job, which means that the service parameters might change over and over again.

It makes the service definition a little tricky. Imagine how many times we would have to refactor the service until we reach the final structure. Luckily, we can create a service with minimal configuration. Introduced in Symfony 2.8, with autowiring, we can ignore details of the service definition and let Symfony find and handle any dependency for us:

```
services:
    som_service:
        class: some_class
        autowire:true
```

You can read more about it here:

```
https://symfony.com/doc/current/components/dependency_injection/
autowiring.html.
```

Organizing services with tags

One useful configuration feature that can be used in the service settings is a tag. It does not alter a service in any way, rather it provides properties that can be used in services for better organization.

For example, open the `services.yml` file in AppBundle and look at the configuration that SonataUserBundle creates to address the user profile edit form:

```
services:
    mava_user.profile.form.type:
        class: AppBundle\Form\ProfileType
        tags:
            - { name: form.type, alias: mava_user_profile }
```

Now open the `config.yml` file and scroll down to `sonata_user`:

```
sonata_user:
    security_acl: true
    manager_type: orm
    profile:
        form:
            type:      mava_user_profile
```

As you can see, Sonata uses tags to address the Profile Edit form for users. In other words, the alias in the tags parameter defines the name for the form type that is used to edit profile information for users. The same alias value is used in the ProfileType class in the form folder:

```php
<?php
namespace AppBundle\Form;
class ProfileType extends AbstractType
{
    // ...
    public function getBlockPrefix()
    {
        return 'mava_user_profile';
    }
}
```

You can see that the tags keyword doesn't do anything here. Basically, it just provides a name that is used everywhere to address the same concept.

With this concept in mind, it should be obvious how tags organize the other services that we have in `services.yml`:

```
my.listener:
    class: AppBundle\EventListener\Notifier
    tags:
        - { name: doctrine.event_listener, event: postPersist }
```

This one tells another story, something like: hey I am a doctrine `event_listener` service that triggers the `postPersist` method in the `Notifier` class.

Open the `Notifier` class and you will see this method here:

```php
<?php
namespace AppBundle\EventListener;
class Notifier {
// ...
    public function postPersist(LifecycleEventArgs $args)
    {
        $entity = $args->getEntity();
        $this->em = $args->getEntityManager();
        $this->notifyRelatedUsers($entity);
    }
}
```

Summary

This chapter was about understanding that services are nothing more than usual PHP objects that are constructed on demand. We saw that their real power comes from the fact that no memory is allocated to them until they are called and, more importantly, no matter how many instances of them are created, the allocated memory never grows over one instance.

You learned where and how to create the required configurations that a Service Container needs in order to instantiate the services. Decoupling bundles by putting their configurations in the `DependencyInjection` folder was another subject that we studied. Lastly, we saw how to use tags in the service configuration in order to organize them better.

So far, we have used default Symfony commands or commands that come with third-party bundles. In the next chapter, we will see how to create our own commands.

10
Custom User Commands

Have you ever wondered where Symfony's console commands come from? For example, when we install FOSUserBundle, we can use the following command to create a new admin:

```
$bin/console fos:create:user <name> <email> <password> --super-admin
```

To see a complete list of available commands, try this command:

```
$ bin/console list
```

It is really handy because we don't need to log in as an admin to create a new admin; we can proceed to the user admin area, fill in the forms, and set the access level for the newly created user. How is this possible and how can we create more commands?

There are many usages for console commands; we can generate quick reports from the command line and e-mail the result to a specific person (that is, completed projects in the past season or a list of users working in a specific workspace).

In this chapter, you will learn how to create custom commands in order to create tasks, assign them to a specific person, and define the project where the task belongs to, all from the command line.

Creating and registering commands

Technically, a custom command is nothing more than a PHP class defined in the Command folder of your bundle. Like other Symfony naming conventions, the filename for this class should end with Command. So, defining new console commands requires two main steps:

1. Create a command class in the bundle
2. Register this command to let Symfony know about it

As long as we create the command class in the Command folder and follow the required naming conventions, registering happens automatically and we don't need to do anything for this. Let's see how to create the command class itself.

Creating commands for tasks

One way to create tasks in our project is to log in, push the add new task button, and fill in the entries here. Wouldn't it be nice if we could do the same from the command line? If we are allowed to see the command line for a live project, this means that we don't need to deal with the hassle of authentication and authorization. So we can get to the point quickly.

To begin with, create a new Command folder in AppBundle and add the following class to it:

File source: // src/AppBundle/Command/TaskCommand.php

```
namespace CoreBundle\Command;
use Symfony\Component\Console\Input\InputOption;
use Symfony\Component\Console\Input\InputArgument;
use Symfony\Component\Console\Input\InputInterface;
use Symfony\Component\Console\Output\OutputInterface;
use Symfony\Bundle\FrameworkBundle\Command\ContainerAwareCommand;

class TaskCommand extends ContainerAwareCommand
{
    protected function configure()  { }
    protected function execute(
            InputInterface $input,
            OutputInterface $output) {
    }
}
```

There are only two methods in this class. As you may have guessed, the configure() method is the place to define the required settings and input parameters for our command. Let's study this method first.

The configuration part

In our example for the task creation command, the configuration part can be defined as follows:

File source: `// src/AppBundle/Command/TaskCommand.php`

```php
// ...
class TaskCommand extends ContainerAwareCommand
{
    protected function configure()
    {
        $this
        ->setName('mava:task:create')
        ->setDescription('Create and assign a new task')
        ->addArgument(
            'taskName', InputArgument::REQUIRED,
            'The task name'
        )
        ->addArgument(
            'taskDesc', InputArgument::REQUIRED,
            'The task description'
        )
        ->addArgument(
            'taskDueDate', InputArgument::REQUIRED,
            'The task due date'
        )
        ->addArgument(
            'taskStatus', InputArgument::REQUIRED,
            'The task status'
        )
      ->addOption(
            'user', null, InputOption::VALUE_REQUIRED,
            'If set, the task will be assigned to the user'
        )
        ->addOption(
            'project', null, InputOption::VALUE_REQUIRED,
            'Defines which project this task is belonged to'
        );
    }
}
```

The `setName()` and `setDescription()` methods should be obvious. Whatever parameter we define in `setName()` will be used in the console to call the command. What this command does is defined in `setDescription()`.

Basically, we have the following naming convention for commands:

```
bundlename:task:action
```

We have two types of input for console commands. The actual arguments are the ones that create the core inputs of the command (that is, `<task name>`):

```
->addArgument(
    'taskName', InputArgument::REQUIRED,
    'The task name?'
        )
```

Note that the order of arguments in a command matters, but you can use options in the order that you like.

The options that add more power by providing some command-line options (that is, `--user:<user id>`) are as follows:

```
->addOption(
    'user', null, InputOption::VALUE_REQUIRED,
    'If set, the task will be assigned to the user'
)
```

The execution part

Now that we have input arguments and options in place, we need to execute them on demand. The purpose of this command is to create a new task and assign it to someone. This sounds like a SQL query. We can add the query logic to the `execute()` method or we can create a service for this and call this service in our command, which is a better way.

Luckily, we have already set up a service in *Chapter 8, Project Review*. So, let's go to our `Util` folder and create a new method in `Mava.php` for our task creation logic:

File source: `// src/AppBundle/Util/Mava.php`

```
namespace AppBundle\Util;
use Doctrine\ORM\EntityManager;
use AppBundle\Entity\Task;
class Mava
{
//...
    public function createTask(
        $taskName,
        $taskDesc,
```

```
            $taskDueDate,
            $taskStatus,
            $userId = null,
            $projectId = null
        ){
            $task = new Task();
            $task->setTitle($taskName);
            $task->setDescription($taskDesc);
            $task->setDueDate(new \DateTime($taskDueDate));
            $task->setStatus($taskStatus);
            if($projectId) {
                $project =
                    $this->em->getRepository('AppBundle:Project');
                $task->setProject($project->find($project_id));
            }
            if($userId) {
                $user = $this->em->getRepository('AppBundle:User');
                $task->setUser($user->find($useId));
            }
            try {
                $this->em->persist($task);
                $this->em->flush();
                return true;
            } catch (\Exception $e) {
                throw $e;
            }
        }
    }
```

Now we can call this service in our command and benefit from its `createTask()` method:

File source: `// src/AppBundle/Command/TaskCommand.php`

```
class TaskCommand extends ContainerAwareCommand
{
// ...
protected function execute(
    InputInterface $input,
    OutputInterface $output)
    {
        $util = $this->getContainer()->get('mava_util');
        $result = $util->createTask(
            $input->getArgument('taskName'),
            $input->getArgument('taskDesc'),
```

```
                $input->getArgument('taskDueDate'),
                $input->getArgument('taskStatus'),
                $input->getOption('user'),
                $input->getOption('project')
            );
            if ($result){
                $output->writeln("Task created successfully.");
            }



        }
    }
```

As I mentioned earlier, we don't need to worry about defining the service because
`mava_util` has been defined as a service in *Chapter 8, Project Review* already. So, simply
by getting the service container, we can call any service available to our project:

```
util = $this->getContainer()->get('mava_util');
```

At this stage, our command is fully functional and we can run it or see the help
information about it simply using the following command:

$ bin/console mava:task:create --help

The usage of the preceding command is shown as follows:

```
mava:task:create [options] [--] <taskName> <taskDesc> <taskDueDate>
<taskStatus>
```

The argument that should be given is shown as follows:

```
    taskName              The task name
    taskDesc              The task description
    taskDueDate           The task due date
    taskStatus            The task status
```

Lets see the options for the command:

```
    --user=USER           If set, the task will be assigned to the
                          nominated user
    --project=PROJECT     If set, defines which project this task is
                          belonged to
```

So far so good, but this command is not user-friendly yet. In other words, it is okay
for someone who knows about its arguments or can call the - -help option to find
out about the available inputs. Let's make it a little easier to use.

Adding interactivity to commands

If we run our command without any input, we will get a `RuntimeException` error:

```
$ bin/console mava:task:create

  [RuntimeException]
  Not enough arguments.
```

However, we have already seen commands that don't need initial inputs to fulfill their purpose. In *Chapter 1, Installing and Configuring Symfony,* for example, we simply called the following command to generate a whole bundle structure:

```
$ bin/console generate:bundle
```

It wasn't necessary to provide any inputs and yet, along the way, it communicated with us and told us what is needed for the next step to generate the bundle. This is a really nice feature. Let's add it to our command.

Console helpers

Console helpers are services that we can use to add interactivity to our commands. We are going to use the Question helper here. First, we need to add the required classes for different types of questions. So open your command class and add the following lines to it:

File source: `// AppBundle/Command/TaskCommand.php`

```php
//...
use Symfony\Component\Console\Question\Question;
use Symfony\Component\Console\Question\ChoiceQuestion;
use Symfony\Component\Console\Question\ConfirmationQuestion;

class TaskCommand extends ContainerAwareCommand
{
    //...
}
```

Adding interactivity means that the input parameters should be optional. In the `configure()` method, note `InputArgument`:

InputArgument::REQUIRED

Change it to the following:

InputArgument::OPTIONAL

These questions will be asked in the `execute()` method and, based on the answers, we will decide the flow of execution. However, the problem is that if we ask everything in this method, it will get bulky and messy. So let's group the questions into three categories:

- Questions related to input arguments: task, description, due date, and status
- Questions related to input options: user and project
- Confirmation question at the end

All we need to do is define a couple of private variables and methods to deal with each group separately. So the basic structure of our command class would be as follows:

File source: // `AppBundle/Command/TaskCommand.php`

```php
//...
class TaskCommand extends ContainerAwareCommand
{
    //...
    private $helper;
    private $aTask, $aDesc, $aDate, $aStat;
    private $aUser, $aProject;
    private $aConfirm;
    //...
    protected function execute(InputInterface $input, OutputInterface
$output)
    {
        $this->helper = $this->getHelper('question');
        $this->argQs($input, $output);
        $this->optQs($input, $output);
        $this->confirmQ($input, $output);

        if ($this->aConfirm) {
            $this->createTask()?
                $output->writeln("Task created successfully."):
                $output->writeln("Something went wrong!");
        } else {
            return;
        }
    }
```

The process for each method is simple:

1. Get a question helper from the service container.
2. Create a new Question instance.
3. Ask the question and proceed to the next action based on the answer.

For input arguments, we will have the following questions:

File source: // `AppBundle/Command/TaskCommand.php`

```
//...
class TaskCommand extends ContainerAwareCommand
{
    //...
    private function argQs(
      InputInterface $input, OutputInterface $output)
    {
        $helper = $this->helper;
        $qTask = new Question("What is the task name?\n", 'task');
        $this->aTask = $helper->ask($input, $output, $qTask);

        $qDesc = new Question(
            "Please provide a short description:\n",
            'description');
        $this->aDesc = $helper->ask($input, $output, $qDesc);

        $qDate = new Question(
            "What is the due date?\n", '31/12/2017');
        $this->aDate = $helper->ask($input, $output, $qDate);

        $qStat = new ChoiceQuestion(
            "What is the task status?\n",
            ['new', 'in progress', 're opened'],
            0);
        $this->aStat = $helper->ask($input, $output, $qStat);
    }
}
```

Note that for the task status, we have a multiple choice question and the default answer is set to the first option.

This method basically collects user answers and saves them in the private variables for future use. The next method deals with the optional inputs:

```php
// AppBundle/Command/TaskCommand.php
//...
class TaskCommand extends ContainerAwareCommand
{
    //...
    private function optQs(InputInterface $input,
        OutputInterface $output)
    {
        $helper = $this->helper;
        $qUser = new ConfirmationQuestion(
            "Would you like to assign this task to a user?
            (yes/[no]) ", false);
        if($helper->ask($input, $output, $qUser)) {
            $qUserID = new Question("User ID: \n", '1');
            $this->aUser= $helper->ask($input, $output, $qUserID);
        }
        $qProject = new ConfirmationQuestion(
            "Would you like to set the project for this task?
            (yes/[no]) ", false);
        if($helper->ask($input, $output, $qProject)) {
            $qProjectID = new Question("Project ID: \n", '1');
         $this->aProject=$helper->ask($input,$output,$qProjectID);
        }
    }
}
```

The reason that we wrapped the optional input questions in a confirmation question is to give them a nationality feature. In other words, they will be asked only if the user says yes to them.

The last step summarizes the provided answers and asks for task creation confirmation as follows:

File source: // CoreBundle/Command/TaskCommand.php

```php
//...
class TaskCommand extends ContainerAwareCommand
{
    //...
    private function confirmQ(
        InputInterface $input, OutputInterface $output)
    {
```

```
        $helper = $this->helper;
        $output->writeln(
            "======[ SUMMARY ]======\n".
            " Task name: ".$this->aTask."\n".
            " Description: ".$this->aDesc."\n".
            " Due on: ".$this->aDate."\n".
            " Status: ".$this->aStat."\n".
            " User id: ".$this->aUser."\n".
            " project id: ".$this->aProject
        );
        $qConfirm = new ConfirmationQuestion(
            "\n\n\tDo you confirm the task creation? ([yes]/no) ",
            true);
        $this->aConfirm= $helper->ask($input, $output, $qConfirm);
    }
}
```

Now that we have all the questions asked and answers have been collected, we can call the createTask() method and show a success or failure message based on the returned value:

File source: // AppBundle/Command/TaskCommand.php

```
//...
class TaskCommand extends ContainerAwareCommand
{
    //...
    private function createTask()
    {
        $util = $this->getContainer()->get('mava_util');
        $result = $util->createTask(
            $this->aTask, $this->aDesc, $this->aDate,
            $this->aStat, $this->aUser, $this->aProject
        );
        return $result;
    }
```

Summary

In this chapter, you learned about console commands and how to configure and execute them. You learned about the question helper and saw how to use different question classes to add interactivity features to our custom commands. Finally, we saw how to get a custom service (that is, `mava_util`) and benefit from its methods in our custom commands.

There is a lot that we can do to decorate a custom command. Fortunately, Symfony comes with a complete documentation about how to do this, which you can find here:

`http://symfony.com/doc/current/components/console/helpers/index.html.`

11
More about Dev, Test and Prod Environments

This is a short chapter about Symfony environments. We will see how they are different from each other, how we can customize them based on project requirements, and how to create our own environment with its own front controller (that is, `app.php`, `app_dev.php`, and `app_[your env name].php`).

Why do we need different environments?

An environment basically provides running instructions for the same code base. It does not change anything in the code itself. It simply tells Symfony when the code is running, which tools and components should accompany it, and what set of parameters should be used.

The default Symfony environments are **Dev**, **Test**, and **Prod**. As their names suggest, they utilize Symfony tools for our code to run in development, test, and production environments respectively.

So what do they mean and how are they different from each other? For example, when we are developing and testing a web application, we need to get as much debug information as possible to hunt down a thrown exception. Running Symfony's Profiler, Logger, and other tools slows down the overall application performance, but in return provides valuable information that helps us spot and fix the problem.

On the other hand, when the application is fully developed and tested, all we need to do is maximize the performance. So we need to switch to the Prod environment and use its configurations, which are basically to optimize the speed.

The environment configuration file

If we are still using the same code base in different environments, this means that a large part of configurations should be the same in all of them. That's correct. Go to the app/config folder and open any of the config_dev.yml, config_test.yml, or config_prod.yml files.

You will see that the main config file is imported as a resource before any settings:

```
# app/config/config_dev.yml
imports:
  - { resource: config.yml }
#...
```

After this, environment-specific settings follow. This means that we are using the main config.yml settings as the essential configurations for our project and only if there is a new definition for any aspect in the current environment, that definition will override the main config file:

```
# app/config/config.yml
#...
framework:
  router:
    resource: "%kernel.root_dir%/config/routing.yml"
    strict_requirements: ~


# app/config/config_dev.yml
imports:
  - { resource: config.yml }

framework:
  router:
    resource: "%kernel.root_dir%/config/routing_dev.yml"
    strict_requirements: true
  profiler: { only_exceptions: false }
```

Processing configuration files

Okay, so we defined the configuration files based on our needs, but how are they actually accessed? Open app/AppKernel.php and scroll down to the following lines:

```
// app/AppKernel.php
// ...
class AppKernel extends Kernel
```

```
{
  public function registerBundles()
  {
    //...
    if (in_array($this->getEnvironment(),
      array('dev', 'test'))) {
      $bundles[] = new Symfony\Bundle\DebugBundle\DebugBundle();
      $bundles[] = new Symfony\Bundle\WebProfilerBundle\
        WebProfilerBundle();
      $bundles[] = new Sensio\Bundle\DistributionBundle\
        SensioDistributionBundle();
      $bundles[] = new Sensio\Bundle\GeneratorBundle\
        SensioGeneratorBundle();
    }
  //...
  }

  public function registerContainerConfiguration(
    LoaderInterface $loader) {
    $loader->load(
      $this->getRootDir().
      '/config/config_'.
      $this->getEnvironment().
      '.yml');
  }
}
```

As you can see, based on the specific environments (`'dev'` and `'test'`), we first register additional bundles to log and profile the execution flow.

Later, in the `registerContainerConfiguration()` method, we load the related configuration file based on the current environment.

The next question would be, how do we decide the environment we want to be in? The answer is via front controllers. Open web/app_dev.php, for example, and find the following line in it:

```
// web/app_dev.php
// ...
  $kernel = new AppKernel('dev', true);
```

When we instantiate a new application kernel, we set the environment for it as well.

Creating a new environment

Based on what we have seen so far, in order to create a new environment, all we need to do is the following:

1. Define a new configuration file.

2. Create a new front controller for it (in case we need to call it explicitly).

To put it in practice, let's imagine that your web application was successful enough to receive sign ups from all around the world. This means that it is wise to use regional servers for each country instead of serving everyone in the world with the same server.

One way to do this is to define different domains for different regions. Again, the code base stays the same, but configurations for the database, caching, and so on should be different. However, because we (as developers) are working from one specific address and need to find a way to Dev/Test the code from our own location, we can have a front controller for that specific region to see how it works.

Let's create the new config file and save it under the name, `config_region2.yml`, and create a new front controller for it and call it `app_region2.php`.

The config file

The new configuration still uses a lot of settings that have already been defined in `config.yml`, so we import them as a resource:

```
# app/config/config_region2.yml
imports:
    - { resource: config.yml }
    - { resource: parameters_region2.php }
```

However, we need a new set of parameters for our new database. Assuming that we still want to use RDS (the relational database in Amazon Web Services), then we can define them in a `.php` file and access them as follows:

```php
<?php
// app/config/parameters_region2.php
if(@$_ENV['SYMFONY__RDS__HOSTNAME']) {
  $container->setParameter(
    'database_host', $_ENV['SYMFONY__RDS__HOSTNAME']);
  $container->setParameter(
    'database_port', $_ENV['SYMFONY__RDS__PORT']);
  $container->setParameter(
    'database_name', $_ENV['SYMFONY__RDS__DBNAME']);
```

```
$container->setParameter(
    'database_user', $_ENV['SYMFONY__RDS__USER']);
$container->setParameter(
    'database_password', $_ENV['SYMFONY__RDS__PASSWORD']);
}
```

These parameters are accessed via environment variables, so we can define them in Apache config files:

```
<VirtualHost *:80>
    # …
    SetEnv    SYMFONY__RDS__HOSTNAME region2_host
    SetEnv    SYMFONY__RDS__USER user
    SetEnv    SYMFONY__RDS__PASSWORD password
    SetEnv    SYMFONY__RDS__DBNAME database
    SetEnv    SYMFONY__RDS__PORT port
    #...
</VirtualHost>
```

> Note that when these environment variables are parsed inside Symfony, they are converted from SYMFONY__RDS__HOSTNAME to rds.hostname.

Now we need to modify `AppKernel.php` to load this configuration file if it is in the right server. We can do this by checking the environment variables:

```
// app/AppKernel.php
public function registerContainerConfiguration(LoaderInterface
    $loader)
{
    $envParameters = $this->getEnvParameters();
    if (@$envParameters['rds.hostname'] == 'region2_host') {
        $loader->load(__DIR__.'/config/config_region2.yml');
    } else {
        $loader->load(__DIR__.'/config/config_'.$this-
            >getEnvironment().'.yml');
    }
}
```

Now we have a new environment for our new region, which has its own settings.

The front controller

We could ignore `AppKernel.php` modifications if we define an explicit front controller for our new environment. This is good when you want to debug and test the application during development.

Simply take a copy of `web/app_dev.php` and name it `app_region2.php`, and then modify the kernel instantiation line as follows:

```
// web/app_region2.php
  //...
  $kernel = new AppKernel('region2', true);
  //...
```

In `AppKernel()`, the second parameter is a flag that indicates whether we want to see debug features (debug toolbar, profiler, and so on) in the new environment or not.

Having an explicit front controller gives us the possibility of defining and adding extra features to our controller without disturbing the Prod environment.

Summary

In this chapter, you learned about the Symfony environments and how they interact with their own configuration files. We saw how to define a new environment by setting the variable values via the Linux environment variables. At the end, we created a new front controller to call our newly created environment explicitly.

In the next chapter, we will discuss caching concepts and how they are beneficial to our project.

12
Caching in Symfony

In this chapter, you are going to learn about performance improvement using cache. Caching is a vast subject and needs its own book to be covered properly. However, in our Symfony project, we are interested in two types of caches only:

- Application cache
- Database cache

We will see what caching facilities are provided in Symfony by default and how we can use them. Then, we will proceed to what is not in Symfony and what options do we have in order to benefit from caching.

We are going to apply the caching techniques on some methods in our projects and watch the performance improvement.

By the end of this chapter, you will have a firm understanding about the usage of HTTP cache headers in the application layer and how to use in-memory caching libraries and technologies such as Memcached, APC, Redis, and others while caching dynamic contents.

Definition of a cache

A cache is a temporary place that stores contents in order to be served faster when they are needed. Considering that we already have a permanent place on disk to store our web contents (templates, codes, and database tables), a cache sounds like a duplicate storage.

That is exactly what they are. They are duplicates and we need them because, in return for consuming extra space to store the same data, they provide a very fast response to some requests. So this is a very good trade-off between storage and performance.

To give you an example of how good this deal can be, consider the following image. On the left-hand side, we have a usual client/server request/response model, and let's say that the response latency is two seconds and there are only 100 users who hit the same content per hour.

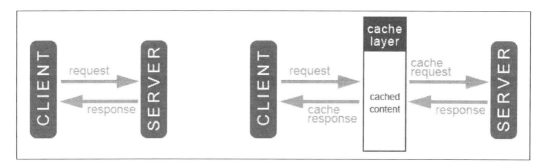

On the right-hand side, however, we have a cache layer that sits between the client and server. What it basically does is it receives the same request and passes it to the server. The server sends a response to the cache and, because this response is new to the cache, it will save a copy (duplicate) of the response and then pass it back to the client. The latency is 2 + 0.2 seconds.

However, it doesn't add up, does it? The purpose of using a cache was to improve the overall performance and reduce the latency. It has already added more delays to the cycle. With this result, how could it possibly be beneficial? The answer is in the next image:

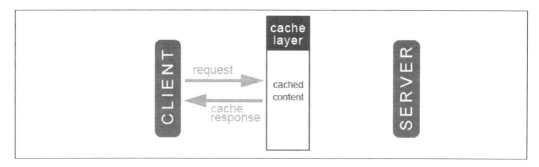

Now, with the response being cached, imagine the same request comes through. (We have about 100 requests/hour for the same content, remember?) This time, the cache layer looks into its space, finds the response, and sends it back to the client without bothering the server. The latency is 0.2 seconds.

Of course, these are only imaginary numbers and situations. However, in the simplest form, this is how a cache works. It might not be very helpful on a low traffic website; however, when we are dealing with thousands of concurrent users on a high traffic website, then we can appreciate the value of caching.

So, according to the preceding images, we can define some terminology and use it in this chapter as we continue. In the first image, when a client asked for that page, it wasn't exited and the cache layer had to store a copy of its contents for future references. This is called cache miss. However, in the second image, we already had a copy of the contents stored in the cache and we benefited from it. This is called cache hit.

Characteristics of a good cache

If you do a quick search, you will find that a good cache is defined as the one that misses only once. In other words, a cache miss happens only if the content has not been requested before. This feature is necessary but not sufficient. To clarify the situation a little more, let's add two more terms here. A cache can be in one of the following states: fresh (has the same contents as the original response) and stale (has the old response's contents that have now changed on the server).

The important question here is how long should a cache be kept for? We have the power to define the freshness of a cache via setting an expiration period. We will see how to do this in the coming sections. However, just because we have this power doesn't mean that we are right about the content's freshness. Consider the following situation:

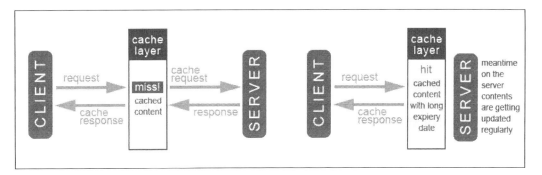

If we cache content for a long time, a cache miss won't happen again (which satisfies the previous definition), but the contents might lose their freshness according to the dynamic resources that might change on the server. To give you an example, nobody likes to read the news from three months ago when they open the BBC website.

Now, we can modify the definition of a good cache as follows:

A cache strategy is considered to be good if a cache miss for the same content happens only once while the cached contents are still fresh.

This means that defining the cache expiry time won't be enough and we need another strategy to keep an eye on cache freshness. This happens via a cache validation strategy. When the server sends a response, we can set the validation rules on the basis of what really matters on the server side, and this way, we can keep the contents stored in cache fresh. We will see how to do this in Symfony soon.

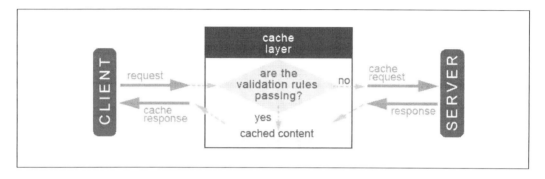

Caches in a Symfony project

In this book, we will focus on two types of caches: the gateway cache (which is called a reverse proxy cache as well) and the doctrine cache. As you may have guessed, the gateway cache deals with all of those HTTP cache headers mentioned in the previous topics. Symfony comes with a very strong gateway cache out of the box. All you need to do is activate it in your front controller, and then start defining your cache expiration and validation strategies in your controllers.

That said, it does not mean that you are forced to use the Symfony cache only. If you prefer other reverse proxy cache libraries (that is, Varnish or Django), you are welcome to use them. The caching configurations in Symfony are transparent so you don't need to change a single line in your controllers when you change your caching libraries. Just modify your `config.yml` file and you will be good to go.

However, we all know that caching is not for the application layer and views only. Sometimes, we need to cache any database-related contents as well. For our Doctrine ORM, this includes metadata cache, query cache, and result cache.

Doctrine comes with its own bundle to handle these types of caches and uses a wide range of libraries (APC, Memcached, Redis, and others) to do the job. Again, we don't need to install anything to use this cache bundle. If we have Doctrine installed already, all we need to do is configure something and then all the Doctrine caching power will be at our disposal.

Putting these two caching types together, we will have a big picture to cache our Symfony project:

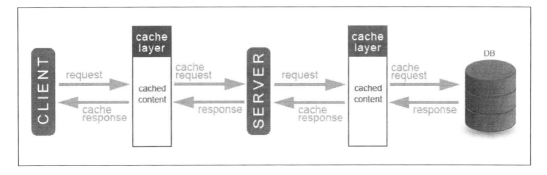

As you can see in this image, we might have a problem with the final cached page. Imagine that we have a static page that might change once a week, and in this page, there are some blocks that might change on a daily or even hourly basis. The user dashboard in our project is a good example.

Thus, if we set the expiration on the gateway cache to one week, we cannot reflect all of those rapid updates in our project and task controllers:

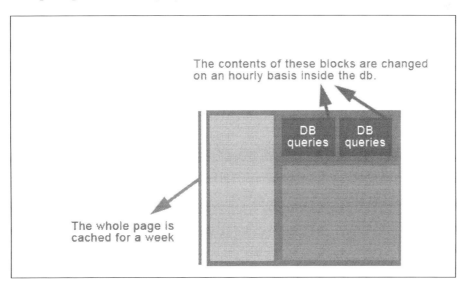

To solve this problem, we can leverage from ESI (Edge Side Includes) in Symfony. Basically, any part of the page that has been defined in an ESI tag can tell its own cache story to the gateway cache. Thus, we can have multiple cache strategies living side by side in a single page. We will see how to use ESI in the coming sections. With this solution, our big picture will look as follows:

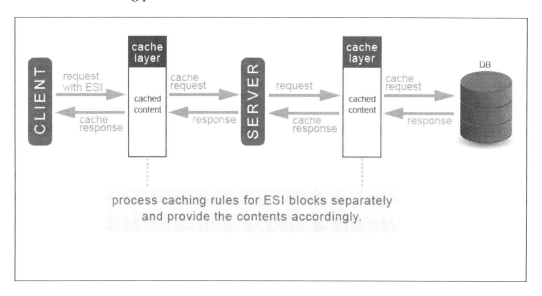

Thus, what we are going to do in this chapter is use the default Symfony and Doctrine caching features for application and model layers, and later I will introduce some popular third-party bundles that you can use for more advanced settings. If you completely understand the principles of caching, moving to other caching bundles will be a breeze.

Key players in the HTTP cache header

Before diving into the Symfony application cache, let's familiarize ourselves with the elements that we need to handle in our cache strategies. To do so, open www.wikipedia.org in your browser, inspect any resource with 304 response code, and ponder on request/response headers in the **Network** tab:

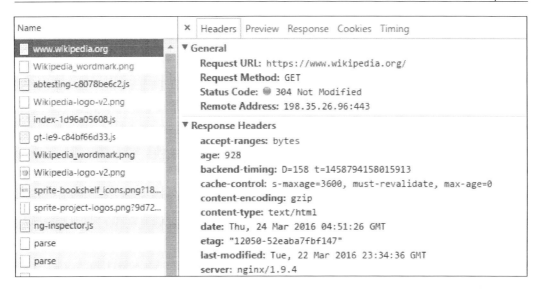

Among the response elements, there are four cache headers that we are interested in the most, **Expires** and **Cache-Control**, which will be used for the expiration model, and **Etag** and **Last-Modified**, which will be used for the validation model.

Apart from these cache headers, we can have variations of the same cache (compressed/uncompressed) via the **Vary** header, and we can define a cache as private (accessible by a specific user) or public (accessible by everyone).

Using the Symfony reverse proxy cache

There is no complicated or lengthy procedure required to activate Symfony's gateway cache. Just open the front controller and uncomment the following lines:

```
// web/app.php
<?php
//...
require_once __DIR__.'/../app/AppKernel.php';
//un comment this line
require_once __DIR__.'/../app/AppCache.php';
$kernel = new AppKernel('prod', false);
$kernel->loadClassCache();
// and this line
$kernel = new AppCache($kernel);
// ...
?>
```

Now, the kernel is wrapped around the **Application Cache** layer, which means that any request coming from the client will pass through this layer first.

Set expiration for dashboard page

Log in to your project, and in the debug toolbar, click on the request section. Then, scroll down to the **Response** header and check the contents:

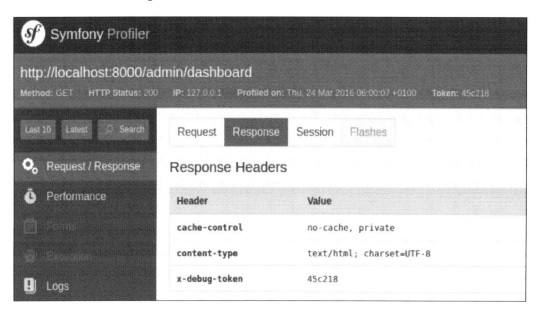

As you can see, only **Cache-Control** is sitting here with some default values among the cache headers that we are interested in.

When you don't set any value for **Cache-Control**, Symfony considers the page contents as private in order to keep them safe.

Now, let's go to the DashboardController and add some gateway cache settings to indexAction:

```php
// src/AppBundle/Controller/DashboardController.php
<?php
namespace AppBundle\Controller;
use Symfony\Bundle\FrameworkBundle\Controller\Controller;
use Symfony\Component\HttpFoundation\Response;

class DashboardController extends Controller
{
    public function indexAction()
```

```
{
    $uId = $this->getUser()->getId();
    $util = $this->get('mava_util');
    $userProjects = $util->getUserProjects($uId);
    $currentTasks= $util->getUserTasks($uId, 'in progress');

    $response = new Response();
    $date = new \DateTime('+2 days');
    $response->setExpires($date);

    return $this->render(
        'CoreBundle:Dashboard:index.html.twig',
        array(
            'currentTasks'  => $currentTasks,
            'userProjects'  => $userProjects
        ),
        $response
    );
    }
}
```

You might have noticed that we didn't change the render method. Instead, we added the response settings as the third parameter of this method. This is a good solution because now we can keep the current template structure and adding new settings won't require any other changes in the code.

However, you might wonder what other options do we have? We can save the whole `$this->render()` method in a variable and assign a response setting to that as follows:

```
// src/AppBundle/Controller/DashboardController.php
<?php
// ...
    $res = $this->render(
            'AppBundle:Dashboard:index.html.twig',
            array(
                'currentTasks'  => $currentTasks,
                'userProjects'  => $userProjects
            )
        );
        $res->setExpires($date);
        return $res;
?>
```

Still looks like a lot of hard work for a simple response header setting. So, let me introduce a better option. We can use the @Cache annotation as follows:

```php
//  src/AppBundle/Controller/DashboardController.php
<?php
namespace AppBundle\Controller;
use Symfony\Bundle\FrameworkBundle\Controller\Controller;
use Sensio\Bundle\FrameworkExtraBundle\Configuration\Cache;

class DashboardController extends Controller
{
    /**
     * @Cache(expires="next Friday")
     */
    public function indexAction()
    {
        $uId = $this->getUser()->getId();
        $util = $this->get('mava_util');
        $userProjects = $util->getUserProjects($uId);
        $currentTasks= $util->getUserTasks($uId, 'in progress');

        return $this->render(
            'AppBundle:Dashboard:index.html.twig', array(
            'currentTasks'  => $currentTasks,
            'userProjects'  => $userProjects
        ));
    }
}
```

Have you noticed that the Response object is completely removed from the code? With the annotation, all the response headers are sent internally, which helps keep the original code clean. Now that's what I call zero-fee maintenance. Let's check our response headers in the Symfony's debug toolbar and see what they look like:

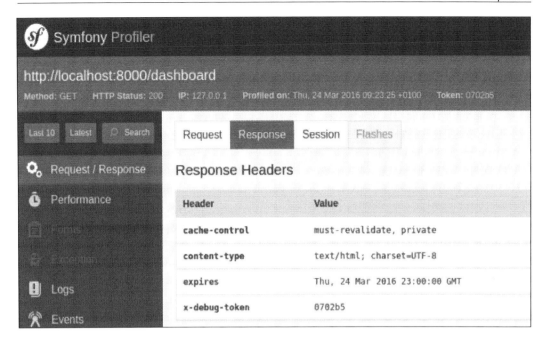

The good thing about the `@Cache` annotation is it can be nested. Imagine that you have a controller full of actions. You want all of them to have a shared maximum age of half an hour, except one that is supposed to be private and should expire in five minutes. That sounds like a lot of code if you are going to use Response objects directly. However, with an annotation, it will be as simple as this:

```php
<?php
//...
/**
 * @Cache(smaxage="1800", public="true")
 */
class DashboardController extends Controller
{
    public function firstAction()  { //... }
    public function secondAction() { //... }

    /**
     * @Cache(expires="300", public="false")
     */
    public function lastAction() { //... }
}
```

The annotation defined before the `Controller` class will apply to every single action, unless we explicitly add a new annotation for an action.

Validation strategy

In the previous example, we set the expiry period for very long. This means that if a new task is assigned to the user, it won't show up in his dashboard because of the wrong caching strategy. To fix this issue, we can validate the cache before using it.

There are two ways for validation:

- We can check the content's date via the **Last-Modified** header: In this technique, we certify the freshness of contents via the time it has been modified. In other words, if we keep track of the dates and times of each change on a resource, then we can simply compare that date with the cache's date and find out if it is still fresh.

- We can use the **Etag** header as a unique content signature: The other solution is to generate a unique string based on the contents and evaluate the cache's freshness based on its signature.

We are going to try both of them in the dashboard controller and see them in action.

Using the right validation header is totally dependent on the current code. In some actions, calculating modified dates is way easier than creating a digital footprint, while in others, going through the date and time function might look costly. Of course, there are situation where generating both headers are critical. So creating it is totally dependent on the code base and what you are going to achieve.

As you can see, we have two entities in the index action and considering the current code, generating the **Etag** looks practical. So the validation header will look as follows:

```php
// src/AppBundle/Controller/DashboardController.php
<?php

//...
class DashboardController extends Controller
{
    /**
     * @Cache(ETag="userProjects ~ finishedTasks")
     */
    public function indexAction() { //... }
}
```

The next time a request arrives, the cache layer looks into the `Etag` value in the controller, compares it with its own `Etag`, and calls the `indexAction()`. Only there is a difference between these two.

How to mix expiration and validation strategies

Imagine that we want to keep the cache fresh for ten minutes and simultaneously keep an eye on any changes over user projects or finished tasks. It is obvious that tasks won't finish every ten minutes and it is far beyond reality to expect changes in the project status during that period.

So what we can do to make our caching strategy efficient is combine expiration and validation and apply them to the dashboard controller as follows:

```php
// src/CoreBundle/Controller/DashboardController.php
<?php
//...
/**
 * @Cache(expires="600")
 */
class DashboardController extends Controller
{
    /**
     * @Cache(ETag="userProjects ~ finishedTasks")
     */
    public function indexAction() { //... }
}
```

Keep in mind that expiration has a higher priority over validation. In other words, the cache is fresh for 10 minutes, regardless of the validation status. So when you visit your dashboard for the first time, a new cache plus a 302 response (not modified) is generated automatically and you will hit the cache for the next 10 minutes.

However, what happens after 10 minutes is a little different. Now, the expiration status is not satisfying; thus, the HTTP flow falls into the validation phase and in case nothing happened to the finished tasks status or your project status, then a new expiration period is generated and you hit the cache again.

However, if there is any change in your tasks or project status, then you will hit the server to get the real response, and a new cache from the response's contents, expiration period, and **Etag** are generated and stored in the cache layer for future references.

Doctrine cache

Using a cache on the model layer is a different story. It does not do this with Symfony out of the box and needs a little bit of effort to install, configure, and use it in our code.

I'm going to explain how to use Doctrine cache in our project because it covers all the basic needs for the caching. Later, I will introduce a more sophisticated bundle that comes with a complete documentation for more advanced caching needs.

First, ensure that you have DoctrineCacheBundle installed and added to your kernel as usual:

```
composer require doctrine/doctrine-cache-bundle

// app/AppKernel.php
public function registerBundles()
{
    // ...
    $bundles[] =
    // ...
new Doctrine\Bundle\DoctrineCacheBundle\DoctrineCacheBundle();
    return $bundles;
}
```

Now, we need to set the right configuration for this bundle. DoctrineCacheBundle has a very useful interface to benefit from all major caching libraries.

The following cache libraries are supported in the current version of DoctrineCacheBundle:

- `ApcCache` (requires ext/apc)
- `ArrayCache` (in memory, lifetime of the request)
- `FilesystemCache` (not optimal for high concurrency)
- `MemcacheCache` (requires ext/memcache)
- `MemcachedCache` (requires ext/memcached)
- `PhpFileCache` (not optimal for high concurrency)
- `RedisCache.php` (requires ext/phpredis)
- `WinCacheCache.php` (requires ext/wincache)
- `XcacheCache.php` (requires ext/xcache)
- `ZendDataCache.php` (requires Zend Server Platform)

In this project, we are going to use APC to cache the metadata and queries, and we are going to use Memcached to cache the results.

Ensure that you have installed the APC (php.net) and Memcached (memcached.org) extensions already.

Open the `config.yml` file and add the following configurations to it:

```
# app/config/config.yml
doctrine:
    # ...
    orm:
        entity_managers:
            default:
            metadata_cache_driver: apc
                query_cache_driver: apc
                result_cache_driver:
                    type: memcached
                    host: localhost
                    port: 11211
                    instance_class: Memcached
```

As you can see, we have three types of caches when it is about the model layer. The metadata information can be in any form. As you saw, all the entities in this project use the annotation format. As we don't want to pass this information with every single request, we can cache them and speed up the process. The metadata cache is in charge of doing this.

Queries are another time-consuming part in each request. As we are using DQL, it takes a little bit of effort to convert each query to a proper SQL equivalent. They don't change very often; thus, we can cache them using a query cache and improve the performance noticeably.

Perhaps the most efficient cache in the database is the result cache. This is when we can feel the real benefits of caching because all the required steps to search, fetch, and hydrate records will be summarized in one prepared piece of data and fed to the client as soon as a request for it arrives.

Consider the Project repository. With the preceding configuration in place, we can apply the required caching as follows:

```
// src/CoreBundle/Entity/ProjectRepositiry.php
<?php
// ...
class ProjectRepository extends EntityRepository
{
```

```
    public function getAllProjects($workSpace_id){
        $q = $this->createQueryBuilder('p')
            ->where('p.workspace = :workSpace_id')
            ->setParameter('workSpace_id', $workSpace_id)
            ->getQuery();

    // this is where above DQL coverted to a SQL and cached
    $q->useQueryCache();

    // this is where result will be cached and ready to be
        // provided for the coming queries in the next 30 minutes
    $q->useResultCache (true, 1800);
        return $q->getResult();
    }
}
```

Putting it all together

So now we have the required setup for gateway cache (or reverse proxy cache) and Doctrine cache. Let's see how we can apply both of them to a specific page.

Let's say we are inside the project page; some parts of it rarely change, such as the project title and descriptions, and some parts of it change a lot, such as new tasks, finished tasks, and current tasks.

Let Doctrine take care of the required metadata, query, and result caches on the database side and feed them to the template. We can define a relatively long expiry period for the page itself and feed it to the gateway cache. However, there is a problem here.

As the dynamic parts of the page change faster than other parts, we won't be able to see the real updates to that page.

If we try to fix the problem by making the expiry time shorter and adding a validation strategy, we will have another problem. As the page will be modified more often, the gateway cache states will turn stale more than they should and add overhead to the page. In other words, caching under these circumstances won't speed up the page load, rather it will slow down the whole request/response life cycle.

So what is the solution here? The answer is Edge Side Includes (ESI).

ESI for selective caching

Here is the definition of ESI according to Wikipedia:

> *"Edge Side Includes or ESI is a small markup language for edge level dynamic web content assembly. The purpose of ESI is to tackle the problem of web infrastructure scaling. Dynamic content creates a problem for caching systems. To overcome this problem a group of companies developed the ESI specification and submitted it to the W3C for approval."*
>
> *- Wikipedia*

In simple words, we can use ESI to define independent caching rules for any section of each page. Again, Symfony comes with out-of-the-box support for the ESI feature. We don't need to install anything to use ESI in our project. All we need to do is uncomment the following line in config.yml:

```
# app/config/config.yml
# ...
framework:
    esi:
```

Then, we need to wrap the part of the template that we want to have a different caching strategy for in an ESI renderer. Thanks to Twig, we can easily do this as follows:

```
# src/Resources/views/Dashboard/index.html.twig
# ...
{{ render_esi(controller('CoreBundle:Task:index')) }}
```

Now, all we need to do is go to indexAction in the TaskController and set a desired caching rule for it:

```php
// src/CoreBundle/Controller/TaskController.php
<?php
//...
class TaskController extends Controller
{
    /**
     * @Cache(smaxage="120")
     */
    public function indexAction() { //... }
}
```

Sophisticated bundles

What was offered in this chapter was a basic understanding and usage of caching strategies. There are far more advanced bundles, which are built on top of principles and offer way more sophisticated solutions for caching strategies.

If you mastered the basics and feel confident proceeding to the next level, I recommend FOSHttpCacheBundle for gateway caching and LswMemcacheBundle for doctrine caching.

Summary

In this chapter, you learned about the basics of gateway and Doctrine caching. We saw how to set expiration and validation strategies using HTTP headers such as cache-control, expires, last-modified, and **Etag**. You learned how to set public and private access levels for a cache and use an annotation to define cache rules in the controller.

On the model layer, we studied metadata, query, and result caches and saw how to configure our project using DoctrineCacheBundle to cache database-related contents.

At the end, we saw how we can have different caching rules for the mostly static and mostly dynamic parts of any HTML page.

Index

A

about page
Behavior Driven Development (BDD),
    implementing 85
Given step 86
headless browser, versus zombie
    browser 83
scenario, executing 81, 82
scenario, writing 81
Selenium2 controller, using for
    automated tests 83, 84
Then step 86
user's details, displaying 85-87
user's details scenario, implementing 88
user's details scenario, testing 89, 90
When step 86
acceptance tests
creating 132
AliceBundle 147, 148
Amazon Web Services (AWS) 38-40
Apache
installing 45
Apache Ant
using 58
AppBundle
versus custom bundles 22, 23
assets
managing 174, 175
organizing 173, 174
attachment feature
adding, to Task entity 202, 203
authentication 139, 140
authorization 140

autowiring
service, creating 223
service, loading 223
URL 223

B

backend logo
modifying 191
base template
modifying 176-178
Behat
about 76, 77
configuring 77, 78
Gherkin 80
installing 77, 78
Behavior Driven Development (BDD)
about 76
comparing, with Test Driven
    Development (TDD) 76
implementing, for about page 85
implementing, with Codeception 121
Bootstrap 180
build process
executing 69, 70
GitHub, used for alerting Jenkins 70
orchestrating 58-62
reference link 58
bundle
anatomy 16-18
best practices 21
generating 18-21
installing 29, 30

business logic
  about 103
  features 120, 121
  location 106
  scenarios 120, 121

C

cache
  about 245-247
  characteristics 247
  doctrine cache 248
  gateway cache 248
  in Symfony project 248-250
Cache Hit 247
Cache Miss 247
Codeception
  about 76, 92, 93
  acceptance test, creating 132, 133
  Behavior Driven Development (BDD),
      implementing 121
  bootstrapping 93, 94
  database, dropping 126, 127
  database, recreating 126, 127
  database, setting up for test
      environment 125
  error handling 134
  functional test, creating 122, 123
  functional test, executing 131
  installing 93
  missing code, developing 123, 124
  showAction() method,
      implementing 130, 131
  Test Driven Development (TDD),
      implementing 121
  testers 97, 98
  tests, adding 98, 99
  tests, executing 99, 100
  test suits 95-97
  unit tests, creating 124-130
  unit tests, executing 131
CodeSniffer
  using 58
commands
  configuration 229, 230
  console helpers 233-237
  creating 227

  creating, for tasks 228
  execution 230-232
  interactivity, adding 233
  registering 227
commenting system
  dashboard page, creating 193, 194
Composer
  about 6, 7
  commands 8
  downloading 7
  used, for installing Symfony 9, 10
conditional templates
  creating 25, 26
configuration files
  processing 240, 241
console helpers
  about 233
  using 233-237
Content Management Systems (CMS) 2
Continuous Integration (CI)
  about 37
  importance 38
  need for 72
controllers
  using, with dynamic templates 32, 33
Controller/View interaction 24, 25
**Create, Read, Update, and Delete
    (CRUD)**
  about 26
  generating 169-171
curl 7
custom bundles
  versus AppBundle 22, 23
custom environment
  config file, defining 242, 243
  creating 242
  front controller, defining 244

D

dashboard page
  creating 193, 194
  Dashboard controller,
      implementing 200, 201
  expiration, setting 252-255
  feature file, creating for finished
      tasks block 195-197

finished tasks block, implementing 197-200
statistics about tasks, displaying 194
template, using 186, 187
database
 configurations, checking 26, 27
 dropping 126, 127
 recreating 126, 127
 setting up, for test environment 125
data fixtures
 AliceBundle 147
 Alice, relationship with 149, 150
 creating 30, 31, 116-120
 creating, Alice used 148, 149
 generating 147
 loading 31, 32
 login redirection, setting up 150
Dependency Injection Container
 about 220, 221
 URL 221
Dev environment 239
Doctrine annotation
 URL 29
doctrine cache
 about 248, 258, 259
 implementing 260
Doctrine extensions
 URL 210
Doctrine's events
 URL 210
dynamic templates
 controllers, using 32, 33
 creating 26

E

Edge Side Includes (ESI)
 about 261
 for selective caching 261
Elastic Compute Cloud (EC2)
 about 40
 instance, creating 41-45
Enhanced Entity-Relation Diagram 108
entity
 adding 109, 110
 generating 27-29, 115
 or Model creation, selecting
  between 104, 105

Entity Relationship Diagrams (ERDs)
 about 107
 creating, MySQL Workbench used 107-109
 tables, creating 112-114
 URL 107
entity relationships
 building 106, 107
environment configuration file 240
environments
 Dev 239
 need for 239
 Prod 239
 Test 239
event dispatchers 212
event listeners 212
events 212

F

Faker
 URL 149
feature files
 defining 91, 92
 prioritizing 91, 92
files
 uploading, with
  SonataMediaBundle 201, 202
forms
 modifying 171, 172
Forward Engineering 112
FOSUserBundle
 configurations, adding 143
 installation, checking 165
 integrating, to admin area 160
 routes, adding 143
 routes, updating 162, 163
 security, setting 142, 143, 164
 simple road test 145-147
 SonataUserBundle, configuring 161
 SonataUserBundle in charge,
  putting 166-168
 SonataUserBundle, installing 160
 tables, adding 144
 users, handling with 140, 141
front controller
 defining, for custom environment 244

functional test
creating 122, 123, 132

G

gateway cache
about 248
expiration and validation strategies,
    implementing together 257
expiration, setting for dashboard
    page 252-255
implementing 260
using 251
validation strategy 256
Gherkin 80
GitHub
used, for alerting Jenkins 70, 71
Goutte 82

H

headless browser
versus zombie browser 83
HTTP cache header 250

J

JavaScript Object Notation (JSON) 14
Jenkins
configuring 55, 56
installing 46, 47
job, creating 64-68
plugins, installing 48-52
security, setting up 48-52
URL 58

L

login redirection, data fixtures
Dashboard Controller, creating 152, 153
dashboard, securing 154
tests, creating for new controller 151

M

mava project
about 79, 80
facts, reviewing 106, 107
features 78, 79

menu
configuring 184-186
rendering, in template 186
Minimum Viable Product (MVP) 79, 104
Mink
about 76
acceptance test flow 90
Mink objects
DocumentElement 91
Driver class 90
NodeElement 91
Session object 90
Model creation
or entity creation, selecting
    between 104, 105
Model-View-Controller (MVC) 2, 34, 103
MopaBootstrapBundle
about 180, 181
Bootstrap, configuring 182-184
MySQL
installing 45
MySQL Workbench
about 107
URL 107
used, for creating Entity Relationship
    Diagrams (ERDs) 107-109

N

navigation 179
notification business logic
about 210, 211
event dispatchers, implementing 212
event listeners, implementing 212
events, implementing 212
notification system
adding 207
time tracking properties, adding 208, 209
Notifier event listener
adding 213-215

O

Object Relational Mapper (ORM) 26

P

Packagist
  about 7
  URL 8, 58
PHP
  installing 45
PhpMyAdmin 126
PHP tools
  installing 56-58
  reference link 57
  Symfony, using 58
PHPUnit 76
Prod environment 239
Project entity
  relationship between, Team and
      User entity 204-207

R

relationship
  adding 111, 112
request/response life cycle 13-16
reverse proxy cache. *See* **gateway cache**

S

selective caching
  with Edge Side Includes (ESI) 261
Selenium2
  about 83
  URL 83, 84
  using, for automated tests 83, 84
separation of concerns (SoC) 104
service
  avoiding, inside bundle 222, 223
  benefits 218
  calling 219, 220
  configuring 220
  creating 218
  creating, via autowiring 223
  loading, via autowiring 223
  organizing, with tags 224, 225
Service-Oriented Architecture
  (SOA) 103, 217

Simple Email Service (SES)
  about 53
  Jenkins, configuring 55, 56
  setting up 53-55
Software as a Service (SaaS) 38
software designing
  Bottom-UP approach 107
  Top-Down approach 107
Sonata
  admin feature for entities with relations,
      creating 159
  bundle, configuring 155, 156
  bundle, installing 155, 156
  contents, adding to dashboard 156-158
  project 154, 155
SonataMediaBundle
  attachment feature, adding to
      Task entity 202, 203
  files, uploading 201, 202
  URL 202
Sonata Project
  URL 120
SonataUserBundle
  configuring 161
  installing 160
sophisticated bundles 262
Symfony
  authentication 139
  authorization 140
  future 3
  influence 2, 3
  installation, checking 12
  installation methods 4
  installing, via Composer 9, 10
  need for 1, 2
  road map 11
  security, organizing 138, 139
  URL 2
  using 58

T

tables
  creating, from Entity Relationship
      Diagrams (ERDs) 112-114

tags
    used, for organizing service 224, 225
Task entity
    attachment feature, adding 202, 203
tasks
    commands, creating 228
Team entity
    creating 203
    relationship between, Project and User
        entity 204-207
templates
    bundles, installing 29, 30
    conditional templates, creating 25, 26
    Controller/View interaction 24, 25
    database configurations, checking 26, 27
    dynamic templates, creating 26
    entity, generating 27-29
    organizing 175
    overriding 188
    profile-related templates 188-191
Test Driven Development (TDD)
    about 76
    comparing, with BDD 76
    implementing, with Codeception 121

Test environment 239
TWIG
    about 23
    used, for creating templates 23, 24

U

unit tests
    creating 124-132
User Acceptance Test (UAT) 132
user dashboard 169
User entity
    relationship between, Team and Project
        entity 204-207

V

VirtualBox
    URL 3

Z

zombie browser
    versus headless browser 83

Made in the USA
Middletown, DE
03 February 2017